C-1963 CAREER EXAMINATION SERIES

This is your
PASSBOOK for...

Transit Electrical Helper Series

Test Preparation Study Guide
Questions & Answers

COPYRIGHT NOTICE

This book is SOLELY intended for, is sold ONLY to, and its use is RESTRICTED to individual, bona fide applicants or candidates who qualify by virtue of having seriously filed applications for appropriate license, certificate, professional and/or promotional advancement, higher school matriculation, scholarship, or other legitimate requirements of education and/or governmental authorities.

This book is NOT intended for use, class instruction, tutoring, training, duplication, copying, reprinting, excerption, or adaptation, etc., by:

1) Other publishers
2) Proprietors and/or Instructors of "Coaching" and/or Preparatory Courses
3) Personnel and/or Training Divisions of commercial, industrial, and governmental organizations
4) Schools, colleges, or universities and/or their departments and staffs, including teachers and other personnel
5) Testing Agencies or Bureaus
6) Study groups which seek by the purchase of a single volume to copy and/or duplicate and/or adapt this material for use by the group as a whole without having purchased individual volumes for each of the members of the group
7) Et al.

Such persons would be in violation of appropriate Federal and State statutes.

PROVISION OF LICENSING AGREEMENTS – Recognized educational, commercial, industrial, and governmental institutions and organizations, and others legitimately engaged in educational pursuits, including training, testing, and measurement activities, may address request for a licensing agreement to the copyright owners, who will determine whether, and under what conditions, including fees and charges, the materials in this book may be used them. In other words, a licensing facility exists for the legitimate use of the material in this book on other than an individual basis. However, it is asseverated and affirmed here that the material in this book CANNOT be used without the receipt of the express permission of such a licensing agreement from the Publishers. Inquiries re licensing should be addressed to the company, attention rights and permissions department.

All rights reserved, including the right of reproduction in whole or in part, in any form or by any means, electronic or mechanical, including photocopying, recording, or by any information storage and retrieval system, without permission in writing from the Publisher.

Copyright © 2024 by
National Learning Corporation

212 Michael Drive, Syosset, NY 11791
(516) 921-8888 • www.passbooks.com
E-mail: info@passbooks.com

PUBLISHED IN THE UNITED STATES OF AMERICA

PASSBOOK® SERIES

THE *PASSBOOK® SERIES* has been created to prepare applicants and candidates for the ultimate academic battlefield – the examination room.

At some time in our lives, each and every one of us may be required to take an examination – for validation, matriculation, admission, qualification, registration, certification, or licensure.

Based on the assumption that every applicant or candidate has met the basic formal educational standards, has taken the required number of courses, and read the necessary texts, the *PASSBOOK® SERIES* furnishes the one special preparation which may assure passing with confidence, instead of failing with insecurity. Examination questions – together with answers – are furnished as the basic vehicle for study so that the mysteries of the examination and its compounding difficulties may be eliminated or diminished by a sure method.

This book is meant to help you pass your examination provided that you qualify and are serious in your objective.

The entire field is reviewed through the huge store of content information which is succinctly presented through a provocative and challenging approach – the question-and-answer method.

A climate of success is established by furnishing the correct answers at the end of each test.

You soon learn to recognize types of questions, forms of questions, and patterns of questioning. You may even begin to anticipate expected outcomes.

You perceive that many questions are repeated or adapted so that you can gain acute insights, which may enable you to score many sure points.

You learn how to confront new questions, or types of questions, and to attack them confidently and work out the correct answers.

You note objectives and emphases, and recognize pitfalls and dangers, so that you may make positive educational adjustments.

Moreover, you are kept fully informed in relation to new concepts, methods, practices, and directions in the field.

You discover that you are actually taking the examination all the time: you are preparing for the examination by "taking" an examination, not by reading extraneous and/or supererogatory textbooks.

In short, this PASSBOOK®, used directedly, should be an important factor in helping you to pass your test.

TRANSIT ELECTRICAL HELPER SERIES

WHAT THE JOB INVOLVES:

Transit Electrical Helpers assist maintainers and supervisory employees in the installation, maintenance, testing and repair of electrical, electromechanical and electronic equipment in various Transit Authority departments; drive motor vehicles to and from work assignments; keep necessary records and write reports; and perform related work.

Signal Maintainer Trainees, under close supervision, receive a course of training both in the classroom and on the job, leading to qualification and competency as a Signal Maintainer in the installation maintenance and repair of electrical and electronic equipment in the Maintenance of Way Division; and perform other related work.

Under direct supervision, they assist maintainers and maintenance supervisors with their work in one of the following areas:

1. In Signal Maintenance, they assist Signal Maintainers and Maintenance Supervisors (Signals) with their work on railroad signal apparatus, including signals, automatic train stops, electronic control systems, track circuit equipment, compressors, interlocking machines, related apparatus and asbestos containing material.
2. In Lighting Maintenance, they assist Light Maintainers and Maintenance Supervisors (Lighting) in the maintenance, installation, inspection, testing, alteration and repair of lighting and related equipment.
3. In Electronic Equipment Maintenance, they assist Electronic Equipment Maintainers and Maintenance Supervisors (Electronic Equipment) with their work on electronic communications, closed circuit television and control systems and equipment.
4. In Escalator and Elevator Maintenance, they assist Transit Electro-Mechanical Maintainers and Maintenance Supervisors (Elevators and Escalators) with their work on elevators, escalators, electrically operated drawbridges and all related electrical and mechanical equipment
5. In Ventilation and Drainage Maintenance, they assist Transit Electro-Mechanical Maintainers and Maintenance Supervisors (Ventilation and Drainage) in the maintenance and repair of ventilation and drainage systems, including fans, blowers, compressors, pumps, sewage ejectors and related equipment.
6. In Power Distribution (Third Rail) Maintenance, they assist Power Distribution Maintainers and Maintenance Supervisors (Power Distribution) with their work on contact rail power distribution systems, including positive and negative cables, rail connections, circuit breakers and related equipment.
7. In Electrical Power Maintenance, they assist Power Maintainers - Group B, Power Cable Maintainers and Maintenance Supervisors (Electrical Power) in the maintenance and repair of mercury arc and silicon rectifiers, rotary converters, high tension switch gear, automatic relay panels and circuits, power cables and auxiliary equipment and accessories, and asbestos-containing material; and drive a truck.
8. In Telephone Maintenance, they assist Telephone Maintainers and Maintenance Supervisors (Telephones) with their work on telephones, intercom systems, emergency alarms, fire alarms, cables, electronic and other communications systems and asbestos-containing material.

THE TEST

The multiple-choice test may include questions on electrical work and equipment in the following areas: basic electrical theory; proper selection and use of tools, instruments and materials; safe, proper and efficient work practices; reading and interpreting blueprints and drawings; performing job related calculations; keeping records; and other related areas.

HOW TO TAKE A TEST

I. YOU MUST PASS AN EXAMINATION

A. WHAT EVERY CANDIDATE SHOULD KNOW

Examination applicants often ask us for help in preparing for the written test. What can I study in advance? What kinds of questions will be asked? How will the test be given? How will the papers be graded?

As an applicant for a civil service examination, you may be wondering about some of these things. Our purpose here is to suggest effective methods of advance study and to describe civil service examinations.

Your chances for success on this examination can be increased if you know how to prepare. Those "pre-examination jitters" can be reduced if you know what to expect. You can even experience an adventure in good citizenship if you know why civil service exams are given.

B. WHY ARE CIVIL SERVICE EXAMINATIONS GIVEN?

Civil service examinations are important to you in two ways. As a citizen, you want public jobs filled by employees who know how to do their work. As a job seeker, you want a fair chance to compete for that job on an equal footing with other candidates. The best-known means of accomplishing this two-fold goal is the competitive examination.

Exams are widely publicized throughout the nation. They may be administered for jobs in federal, state, city, municipal, town or village governments or agencies.

Any citizen may apply, with some limitations, such as the age or residence of applicants. Your experience and education may be reviewed to see whether you meet the requirements for the particular examination. When these requirements exist, they are reasonable and applied consistently to all applicants. Thus, a competitive examination may cause you some uneasiness now, but it is your privilege and safeguard.

C. HOW ARE CIVIL SERVICE EXAMS DEVELOPED?

Examinations are carefully written by trained technicians who are specialists in the field known as "psychological measurement," in consultation with recognized authorities in the field of work that the test will cover. These experts recommend the subject matter areas or skills to be tested; only those knowledges or skills important to your success on the job are included. The most reliable books and source materials available are used as references. Together, the experts and technicians judge the difficulty level of the questions.

Test technicians know how to phrase questions so that the problem is clearly stated. Their ethics do not permit "trick" or "catch" questions. Questions may have been tried out on sample groups, or subjected to statistical analysis, to determine their usefulness.

Written tests are often used in combination with performance tests, ratings of training and experience, and oral interviews. All of these measures combine to form the best-known means of finding the right person for the right job.

II. HOW TO PASS THE WRITTEN TEST

A. NATURE OF THE EXAMINATION

To prepare intelligently for civil service examinations, you should know how they differ from school examinations you have taken. In school you were assigned certain definite pages to read or subjects to cover. The examination questions were quite detailed and usually emphasized memory. Civil service exams, on the other hand, try to discover your present ability to perform the duties of a position, plus your potentiality to learn these duties. In other words, a civil service exam attempts to predict how successful you will be. Questions cover such a broad area that they cannot be as minute and detailed as school exam questions.

In the public service similar kinds of work, or positions, are grouped together in one "class." This process is known as *position-classification*. All the positions in a class are paid according to the salary range for that class. One class title covers all of these positions, and they are all tested by the same examination.

B. FOUR BASIC STEPS

1) Study the announcement

How, then, can you know what subjects to study? Our best answer is: "Learn as much as possible about the class of positions for which you've applied." The exam will test the knowledge, skills and abilities needed to do the work.

Your most valuable source of information about the position you want is the official exam announcement. This announcement lists the training and experience qualifications. Check these standards and apply only if you come reasonably close to meeting them.

The brief description of the position in the examination announcement offers some clues to the subjects which will be tested. Think about the job itself. Review the duties in your mind. Can you perform them, or are there some in which you are rusty? Fill in the blank spots in your preparation.

Many jurisdictions preview the written test in the exam announcement by including a section called "Knowledge and Abilities Required," "Scope of the Examination," or some similar heading. Here you will find out specifically what fields will be tested.

2) Review your own background

Once you learn in general what the position is all about, and what you need to know to do the work, ask yourself which subjects you already know fairly well and which need improvement. You may wonder whether to concentrate on improving your strong areas or on building some background in your fields of weakness. When the announcement has specified "some knowledge" or "considerable knowledge," or has used adjectives like "beginning principles of..." or "advanced ... methods," you can get a clue as to the number and difficulty of questions to be asked in any given field. More questions, and hence broader coverage, would be included for those subjects which are more important in the work. Now weigh your strengths and weaknesses against the job requirements and prepare accordingly.

3) Determine the level of the position

Another way to tell how intensively you should prepare is to understand the level of the job for which you are applying. Is it the entering level? In other words, is this the position in which beginners in a field of work are hired? Or is it an intermediate or advanced level? Sometimes this is indicated by such words as "Junior" or "Senior" in the class title. Other jurisdictions use Roman numerals to designate the level – Clerk I, Clerk II, for example. The word "Supervisor" sometimes appears in the title. If the level is not indicated by the title, check the description of duties. Will you be working under very close supervision, or will you have responsibility for independent decisions in this work?

4) Choose appropriate study materials

Now that you know the subjects to be examined and the relative amount of each subject to be covered, you can choose suitable study materials. For beginning level jobs, or even advanced ones, if you have a pronounced weakness in some aspect of your training, read a modern, standard textbook in that field. Be sure it is up to date and has general coverage. Such books are normally available at your library, and the librarian will be glad to help you locate one. For entry-level positions, questions of appropriate difficulty are chosen – neither highly advanced questions, nor those too simple. Such questions require careful thought but not advanced training.

If the position for which you are applying is technical or advanced, you will read more advanced, specialized material. If you are already familiar with the basic principles of your field, elementary textbooks would waste your time. Concentrate on advanced textbooks and technical periodicals. Think through the concepts and review difficult problems in your field.

These are all general sources. You can get more ideas on your own initiative, following these leads. For example, training manuals and publications of the government agency which employs workers in your field can be useful, particularly for technical and professional positions. A letter or visit to the government department involved may result in more specific study suggestions, and certainly will provide you with a more definite idea of the exact nature of the position you are seeking.

III. KINDS OF TESTS

Tests are used for purposes other than measuring knowledge and ability to perform specified duties. For some positions, it is equally important to test ability to make adjustments to new situations or to profit from training. In others, basic mental abilities not dependent on information are essential. Questions which test these things may not appear as pertinent to the duties of the position as those which test for knowledge and information. Yet they are often highly important parts of a fair examination. For very general questions, it is almost impossible to help you direct your study efforts. What we can do is to point out some of the more common of these general abilities needed in public service positions and describe some typical questions.

1) General information

Broad, general information has been found useful for predicting job success in some kinds of work. This is tested in a variety of ways, from vocabulary lists to questions about current events. Basic background in some field of work, such as sociology or economics, may be sampled in a group of questions. Often these are principles which have become familiar to most persons through exposure rather than through formal training. It is difficult to advise you how to study for these questions; being alert to the world around you is our best suggestion.

2) Verbal ability

An example of an ability needed in many positions is verbal or language ability. Verbal ability is, in brief, the ability to use and understand words. Vocabulary and grammar tests are typical measures of this ability. Reading comprehension or paragraph interpretation questions are common in many kinds of civil service tests. You are given a paragraph of written material and asked to find its central meaning.

3) Numerical ability

Number skills can be tested by the familiar arithmetic problem, by checking paired lists of numbers to see which are alike and which are different, or by interpreting charts and graphs. In the latter test, a graph may be printed in the test booklet which you are asked to use as the basis for answering questions.

4) Observation

A popular test for law-enforcement positions is the observation test. A picture is shown to you for several minutes, then taken away. Questions about the picture test your ability to observe both details and larger elements.

5) Following directions

In many positions in the public service, the employee must be able to carry out written instructions dependably and accurately. You may be given a chart with several columns, each column listing a variety of information. The questions require you to carry out directions involving the information given in the chart.

6) Skills and aptitudes

Performance tests effectively measure some manual skills and aptitudes. When the skill is one in which you are trained, such as typing or shorthand, you can practice. These tests are often very much like those given in business school or high school courses. For many of the other skills and aptitudes, however, no short-time preparation can be made. Skills and abilities natural to you or that you have developed throughout your lifetime are being tested.

Many of the general questions just described provide all the data needed to answer the questions and ask you to use your reasoning ability to find the answers. Your best preparation for these tests, as well as for tests of facts and ideas, is to be at your physical and mental best. You, no doubt, have your own methods of getting into an exam-taking mood and keeping "in shape." The next section lists some ideas on this subject.

IV. KINDS OF QUESTIONS

Only rarely is the "essay" question, which you answer in narrative form, used in civil service tests. Civil service tests are usually of the short-answer type. Full instructions for answering these questions will be given to you at the examination. But in case this is your first experience with short-answer questions and separate answer sheets, here is what you need to know:

1) Multiple-choice Questions

Most popular of the short-answer questions is the "multiple choice" or "best answer" question. It can be used, for example, to test for factual knowledge, ability to solve problems or judgment in meeting situations found at work.

A multiple-choice question is normally one of three types—
- It can begin with an incomplete statement followed by several possible endings. You are to find the one ending which *best* completes the statement, although some of the others may not be entirely wrong.
- It can also be a complete statement in the form of a question which is answered by choosing one of the statements listed.

- It can be in the form of a problem – again you select the best answer.

Here is an example of a multiple-choice question with a discussion which should give you some clues as to the method for choosing the right answer:

When an employee has a complaint about his assignment, the action which will *best* help him overcome his difficulty is to
   A. discuss his difficulty with his coworkers
   B. take the problem to the head of the organization
   C. take the problem to the person who gave him the assignment
   D. say nothing to anyone about his complaint

In answering this question, you should study each of the choices to find which is best. Consider choice "A" – Certainly an employee may discuss his complaint with fellow employees, but no change or improvement can result, and the complaint remains unresolved. Choice "B" is a poor choice since the head of the organization probably does not know what assignment you have been given, and taking your problem to him is known as "going over the head" of the supervisor. The supervisor, or person who made the assignment, is the person who can clarify it or correct any injustice. Choice "C" is, therefore, correct. To say nothing, as in choice "D," is unwise. Supervisors have and interest in knowing the problems employees are facing, and the employee is seeking a solution to his problem.

2) True/False Questions

The "true/false" or "right/wrong" form of question is sometimes used. Here a complete statement is given. Your job is to decide whether the statement is right or wrong.

SAMPLE: A roaming cell-phone call to a nearby city costs less than a non-roaming call to a distant city.

This statement is wrong, or false, since roaming calls are more expensive.

This is not a complete list of all possible question forms, although most of the others are variations of these common types. You will always get complete directions for answering questions. Be sure you understand *how* to mark your answers – ask questions until you do.

V. RECORDING YOUR ANSWERS

Computer terminals are used more and more today for many different kinds of exams.

For an examination with very few applicants, you may be told to record your answers in the test booklet itself. Separate answer sheets are much more common. If this separate answer sheet is to be scored by machine – and this is often the case – it is highly important that you mark your answers correctly in order to get credit.

An electronic scoring machine is often used in civil service offices because of the speed with which papers can be scored. Machine-scored answer sheets must be marked with a pencil, which will be given to you. This pencil has a high graphite content which responds to the electronic scoring machine. As a matter of fact, stray dots may register as answers, so do not let your pencil rest on the answer sheet while you are pondering the correct answer. Also, if your pencil lead breaks or is otherwise defective, ask for another.

Since the answer sheet will be dropped in a slot in the scoring machine, be careful not to bend the corners or get the paper crumpled.

The answer sheet normally has five vertical columns of numbers, with 30 numbers to a column. These numbers correspond to the question numbers in your test booklet. After each number, going across the page are four or five pairs of dotted lines. These short dotted lines have small letters or numbers above them. The first two pairs may also have a "T" or "F" above the letters. This indicates that the first two pairs only are to be used if the questions are of the true-false type. If the questions are multiple choice, disregard the "T" and "F" and pay attention only to the small letters or numbers.

Answer your questions in the manner of the sample that follows:

32. The largest city in the United States is
    A. Washington, D.C.
    B. New York City
    C. Chicago
    D. Detroit
    E. San Francisco

1) Choose the answer you think is best. (New York City is the largest, so "B" is correct.)
2) Find the row of dotted lines numbered the same as the question you are answering. (Find row number 32)
3) Find the pair of dotted lines corresponding to the answer. (Find the pair of lines under the mark "B.")
4) Make a solid black mark between the dotted lines.

VI. BEFORE THE TEST

Common sense will help you find procedures to follow to get ready for an examination. Too many of us, however, overlook these sensible measures. Indeed, nervousness and fatigue have been found to be the most serious reasons why applicants fail to do their best on civil service tests. Here is a list of reminders:

- Begin your preparation early – Don't wait until the last minute to go scurrying around for books and materials or to find out what the position is all about.
- Prepare continuously – An hour a night for a week is better than an all-night cram session. This has been definitely established. What is more, a night a week for a month will return better dividends than crowding your study into a shorter period of time.
- Locate the place of the exam – You have been sent a notice telling you when and where to report for the examination. If the location is in a different town or otherwise unfamiliar to you, it would be well to inquire the best route and learn something about the building.
- Relax the night before the test – Allow your mind to rest. Do not study at all that night. Plan some mild recreation or diversion; then go to bed early and get a good night's sleep.
- Get up early enough to make a leisurely trip to the place for the test – This way unforeseen events, traffic snarls, unfamiliar buildings, etc. will not upset you.
- Dress comfortably – A written test is not a fashion show. You will be known by number and not by name, so wear something comfortable.

- Leave excess paraphernalia at home – Shopping bags and odd bundles will get in your way. You need bring only the items mentioned in the official notice you received; usually everything you need is provided. Do not bring reference books to the exam. They will only confuse those last minutes and be taken away from you when in the test room.
- Arrive somewhat ahead of time – If because of transportation schedules you must get there very early, bring a newspaper or magazine to take your mind off yourself while waiting.
- Locate the examination room – When you have found the proper room, you will be directed to the seat or part of the room where you will sit. Sometimes you are given a sheet of instructions to read while you are waiting. Do not fill out any forms until you are told to do so; just read them and be prepared.
- Relax and prepare to listen to the instructions
- If you have any physical problem that may keep you from doing your best, be sure to tell the test administrator. If you are sick or in poor health, you really cannot do your best on the exam. You can come back and take the test some other time.

VII. AT THE TEST

The day of the test is here and you have the test booklet in your hand. The temptation to get going is very strong. Caution! There is more to success than knowing the right answers. You must know how to identify your papers and understand variations in the type of short-answer question used in this particular examination. Follow these suggestions for maximum results from your efforts:

1) Cooperate with the monitor

The test administrator has a duty to create a situation in which you can be as much at ease as possible. He will give instructions, tell you when to begin, check to see that you are marking your answer sheet correctly, and so on. He is not there to guard you, although he will see that your competitors do not take unfair advantage. He wants to help you do your best.

2) Listen to all instructions

Don't jump the gun! Wait until you understand all directions. In most civil service tests you get more time than you need to answer the questions. So don't be in a hurry. Read each word of instructions until you clearly understand the meaning. Study the examples, listen to all announcements and follow directions. Ask questions if you do not understand what to do.

3) Identify your papers

Civil service exams are usually identified by number only. You will be assigned a number; you must not put your name on your test papers. Be sure to copy your number correctly. Since more than one exam may be given, copy your exact examination title.

4) Plan your time

Unless you are told that a test is a "speed" or "rate of work" test, speed itself is usually not important. Time enough to answer all the questions will be provided, but this does not mean that you have all day. An overall time limit has been set. Divide the total time (in minutes) by the number of questions to determine the approximate time you have for each question.

5) Do not linger over difficult questions

If you come across a difficult question, mark it with a paper clip (useful to have along) and come back to it when you have been through the booklet. One caution if you do this – be sure to skip a number on your answer sheet as well. Check often to be sure that you have not lost your place and that you are marking in the row numbered the same as the question you are answering.

6) Read the questions

Be sure you know what the question asks! Many capable people are unsuccessful because they failed to *read* the questions correctly.

7) Answer all questions

Unless you have been instructed that a penalty will be deducted for incorrect answers, it is better to guess than to omit a question.

8) Speed tests

It is often better NOT to guess on speed tests. It has been found that on timed tests people are tempted to spend the last few seconds before time is called in marking answers at random – without even reading them – in the hope of picking up a few extra points. To discourage this practice, the instructions may warn you that your score will be "corrected" for guessing. That is, a penalty will be applied. The incorrect answers will be deducted from the correct ones, or some other penalty formula will be used.

9) Review your answers

If you finish before time is called, go back to the questions you guessed or omitted to give them further thought. Review other answers if you have time.

10) Return your test materials

If you are ready to leave before others have finished or time is called, take ALL your materials to the monitor and leave quietly. Never take any test material with you. The monitor can discover whose papers are not complete, and taking a test booklet may be grounds for disqualification.

VIII. EXAMINATION TECHNIQUES

1) Read the general instructions carefully. These are usually printed on the first page of the exam booklet. As a rule, these instructions refer to the timing of the examination; the fact that you should not start work until the signal and must stop work at a signal, etc. If there are any *special* instructions, such as a choice of questions to be answered, make sure that you note this instruction carefully.

2) When you are ready to start work on the examination, that is as soon as the signal has been given, read the instructions to each question booklet, underline any key words or phrases, such as *least, best, outline, describe* and the like. In this way you will tend to answer as requested rather than discover on reviewing your paper that you *listed without describing*, that you selected the *worst* choice rather than the *best* choice, etc.

3) If the examination is of the objective or multiple-choice type – that is, each question will also give a series of possible answers: A, B, C or D, and you are called upon to select the best answer and write the letter next to that answer on your answer paper – it is advisable to start answering each question in turn. There may be anywhere from 50 to 100 such questions in the three or four hours allotted and you can see how much time would be taken if you read through all the questions before beginning to answer any. Furthermore, if you come across a question or group of questions which you know would be difficult to answer, it would undoubtedly affect your handling of all the other questions.

4) If the examination is of the essay type and contains but a few questions, it is a moot point as to whether you should read all the questions before starting to answer any one. Of course, if you are given a choice – say five out of seven and the like – then it is essential to read all the questions so you can eliminate the two that are most difficult. If, however, you are asked to answer all the questions, there may be danger in trying to answer the easiest one first because you may find that you will spend too much time on it. The best technique is to answer the first question, then proceed to the second, etc.

5) Time your answers. Before the exam begins, write down the time it started, then add the time allowed for the examination and write down the time it must be completed, then divide the time available somewhat as follows:
    - If 3-1/2 hours are allowed, that would be 210 minutes. If you have 80 objective-type questions, that would be an average of 2-1/2 minutes per question. Allow yourself no more than 2 minutes per question, or a total of 160 minutes, which will permit about 50 minutes to review.
    - If for the time allotment of 210 minutes there are 7 essay questions to answer, that would average about 30 minutes a question. Give yourself only 25 minutes per question so that you have about 35 minutes to review.

6) The most important instruction is to *read each question* and make sure you know what is wanted. The second most important instruction is to *time yourself properly* so that you answer every question. The third most important instruction is to *answer every question*. Guess if you have to but include something for each question. Remember that you will receive no credit for a blank and will probably receive some credit if you write something in answer to an essay question. If you guess a letter – say "B" for a multiple-choice question – you may have guessed right. If you leave a blank as an answer to a multiple-choice question, the examiners may respect your feelings but it will not add a point to your score. Some exams may penalize you for wrong answers, so in such cases *only*, you may not want to guess unless you have some basis for your answer.

7) Suggestions
    a. Objective-type questions
        1. Examine the question booklet for proper sequence of pages and questions
        2. Read all instructions carefully
        3. Skip any question which seems too difficult; return to it after all other questions have been answered
        4. Apportion your time properly; do not spend too much time on any single question or group of questions

5. Note and underline key words – *all, most, fewest, least, best, worst, same, opposite,* etc.
6. Pay particular attention to negatives
7. Note unusual option, e.g., unduly long, short, complex, different or similar in content to the body of the question
8. Observe the use of "hedging" words – *probably, may, most likely,* etc.
9. Make sure that your answer is put next to the same number as the question
10. Do not second-guess unless you have good reason to believe the second answer is definitely more correct
11. Cross out original answer if you decide another answer is more accurate; do not erase until you are ready to hand your paper in
12. Answer all questions; guess unless instructed otherwise
13. Leave time for review

b. Essay questions
   1. Read each question carefully
   2. Determine exactly what is wanted. Underline key words or phrases.
   3. Decide on outline or paragraph answer
   4. Include many different points and elements unless asked to develop any one or two points or elements
   5. Show impartiality by giving pros and cons unless directed to select one side only
   6. Make and write down any assumptions you find necessary to answer the questions
   7. Watch your English, grammar, punctuation and choice of words
   8. Time your answers; don't crowd material

8) Answering the essay question

Most essay questions can be answered by framing the specific response around several key words or ideas. Here are a few such key words or ideas:

M's: manpower, materials, methods, money, management
P's: purpose, program, policy, plan, procedure, practice, problems, pitfalls, personnel, public relations
   a. Six basic steps in handling problems:
      1. Preliminary plan and background development
      2. Collect information, data and facts
      3. Analyze and interpret information, data and facts
      4. Analyze and develop solutions as well as make recommendations
      5. Prepare report and sell recommendations
      6. Install recommendations and follow up effectiveness

   b. Pitfalls to avoid
      1. *Taking things for granted* – A statement of the situation does not necessarily imply that each of the elements is necessarily true; for example, a complaint may be invalid and biased so that all that can be taken for granted is that a complaint has been registered

2. *Considering only one side of a situation* – Wherever possible, indicate several alternatives and then point out the reasons you selected the best one
3. *Failing to indicate follow up* – Whenever your answer indicates action on your part, make certain that you will take proper follow-up action to see how successful your recommendations, procedures or actions turn out to be
4. *Taking too long in answering any single question* – Remember to time your answers properly

IX. AFTER THE TEST

Scoring procedures differ in detail among civil service jurisdictions although the general principles are the same. Whether the papers are hand-scored or graded by machine we have described, they are nearly always graded by number. That is, the person who marks the paper knows only the number – never the name – of the applicant. Not until all the papers have been graded will they be matched with names. If other tests, such as training and experience or oral interview ratings have been given, scores will be combined. Different parts of the examination usually have different weights. For example, the written test might count 60 percent of the final grade, and a rating of training and experience 40 percent. In many jurisdictions, veterans will have a certain number of points added to their grades.

After the final grade has been determined, the names are placed in grade order and an eligible list is established. There are various methods for resolving ties between those who get the same final grade – probably the most common is to place first the name of the person whose application was received first. Job offers are made from the eligible list in the order the names appear on it. You will be notified of your grade and your rank as soon as all these computations have been made. This will be done as rapidly as possible.

People who are found to meet the requirements in the announcement are called "eligibles." Their names are put on a list of eligible candidates. An eligible's chances of getting a job depend on how high he stands on this list and how fast agencies are filling jobs from the list.

When a job is to be filled from a list of eligibles, the agency asks for the names of people on the list of eligibles for that job. When the civil service commission receives this request, it sends to the agency the names of the three people highest on this list. Or, if the job to be filled has specialized requirements, the office sends the agency the names of the top three persons who meet these requirements from the general list.

The appointing officer makes a choice from among the three people whose names were sent to him. If the selected person accepts the appointment, the names of the others are put back on the list to be considered for future openings.

That is the rule in hiring from all kinds of eligible lists, whether they are for typist, carpenter, chemist, or something else. For every vacancy, the appointing officer has his choice of any one of the top three eligibles on the list. This explains why the person whose name is on top of the list sometimes does not get an appointment when some of the persons lower on the list do. If the appointing officer chooses the second or third eligible, the No. 1 eligible does not get a job at once, but stays on the list until he is appointed or the list is terminated.

X. HOW TO PASS THE INTERVIEW TEST

The examination for which you applied requires an oral interview test. You have already taken the written test and you are now being called for the interview test – the final part of the formal examination.

You may think that it is not possible to prepare for an interview test and that there are no procedures to follow during an interview. Our purpose is to point out some things you can do in advance that will help you and some good rules to follow and pitfalls to avoid while you are being interviewed.

What is an interview supposed to test?

The written examination is designed to test the technical knowledge and competence of the candidate; the oral is designed to evaluate intangible qualities, not readily measured otherwise, and to establish a list showing the relative fitness of each candidate – as measured against his competitors – for the position sought. Scoring is not on the basis of "right" and "wrong," but on a sliding scale of values ranging from "not passable" to "outstanding." As a matter of fact, it is possible to achieve a relatively low score without a single "incorrect" answer because of evident weakness in the qualities being measured.

Occasionally, an examination may consist entirely of an oral test – either an individual or a group oral. In such cases, information is sought concerning the technical knowledges and abilities of the candidate, since there has been no written examination for this purpose. More commonly, however, an oral test is used to supplement a written examination.

Who conducts interviews?

The composition of oral boards varies among different jurisdictions. In nearly all, a representative of the personnel department serves as chairman. One of the members of the board may be a representative of the department in which the candidate would work. In some cases, "outside experts" are used, and, frequently, a businessman or some other representative of the general public is asked to serve. Labor and management or other special groups may be represented. The aim is to secure the services of experts in the appropriate field.

However the board is composed, it is a good idea (and not at all improper or unethical) to ascertain in advance of the interview who the members are and what groups they represent. When you are introduced to them, you will have some idea of their backgrounds and interests, and at least you will not stutter and stammer over their names.

What should be done before the interview?

While knowledge about the board members is useful and takes some of the surprise element out of the interview, there is other preparation which is more substantive. It *is* possible to prepare for an oral interview – in several ways:

1) Keep a copy of your application and review it carefully before the interview

This may be the only document before the oral board, and the starting point of the interview. Know what education and experience you have listed there, and the sequence and dates of all of it. Sometimes the board will ask you to review the highlights of your experience for them; you should not have to hem and haw doing it.

2) Study the class specification and the examination announcement

Usually, the oral board has one or both of these to guide them. The qualities, characteristics or knowledges required by the position sought are stated in these documents. They offer valuable clues as to the nature of the oral interview. For example, if the job involves supervisory responsibilities, the announcement will usually indicate that knowledge of modern supervisory methods and the qualifications of the candidate as a supervisor will be tested. If so, you can expect such questions, frequently in the form of a hypothetical situation which you are expected to solve. NEVER go into an oral without knowledge of the duties and responsibilities of the job you seek.

3) Think through each qualification required

Try to visualize the kind of questions you would ask if you were a board member. How well could you answer them? Try especially to appraise your own knowledge and background in each area, *measured against the job sought*, and identify any areas in which you are weak. Be critical and realistic – do not flatter yourself.

4) Do some general reading in areas in which you feel you may be weak

For example, if the job involves supervision and your past experience has NOT, some general reading in supervisory methods and practices, particularly in the field of human relations, might be useful. Do NOT study agency procedures or detailed manuals. The oral board will be testing your understanding and capacity, not your memory.

5) Get a good night's sleep and watch your general health and mental attitude

You will want a clear head at the interview. Take care of a cold or any other minor ailment, and of course, no hangovers.

What should be done on the day of the interview?

Now comes the day of the interview itself. Give yourself plenty of time to get there. Plan to arrive somewhat ahead of the scheduled time, particularly if your appointment is in the fore part of the day. If a previous candidate fails to appear, the board might be ready for you a bit early. By early afternoon an oral board is almost invariably behind schedule if there are many candidates, and you may have to wait. Take along a book or magazine to read, or your application to review, but leave any extraneous material in the waiting room when you go in for your interview. In any event, relax and compose yourself.

The matter of dress is important. The board is forming impressions about you – from your experience, your manners, your attitude, and your appearance. Give your personal appearance careful attention. Dress your best, but not your flashiest. Choose conservative, appropriate clothing, and be sure it is immaculate. This is a business interview, and your appearance should indicate that you regard it as such. Besides, being well groomed and properly dressed will help boost your confidence.

Sooner or later, someone will call your name and escort you into the interview room. *This is it.* From here on you are on your own. It is too late for any more preparation. But remember, you asked for this opportunity to prove your fitness, and you are here because your request was granted.

What happens when you go in?

The usual sequence of events will be as follows: The clerk (who is often the board stenographer) will introduce you to the chairman of the oral board, who will introduce you to the other members of the board. Acknowledge the introductions before you sit down. Do not be surprised if you find a microphone facing you or a stenotypist sitting by. Oral interviews are usually recorded in the event of an appeal or other review.

Usually the chairman of the board will open the interview by reviewing the highlights of your education and work experience from your application – primarily for the benefit of the other members of the board, as well as to get the material into the record. Do not interrupt or comment unless there is an error or significant misinterpretation; if that is the case, do not hesitate. But do not quibble about insignificant matters. Also, he will usually ask you some question about your education, experience or your present job – partly to get you to start talking and to establish the interviewing "rapport." He may start the actual questioning, or turn it over to one of the other members. Frequently, each member undertakes the questioning on a particular area, one in which he is perhaps most competent, so you can expect each member to participate in the examination. Because time is limited, you may also expect some rather abrupt switches in the direction the questioning takes, so do not be upset by it. Normally, a board member will not pursue a single line of questioning unless he discovers a particular strength or weakness.

After each member has participated, the chairman will usually ask whether any member has any further questions, then will ask you if you have anything you wish to add. Unless you are expecting this question, it may floor you. Worse, it may start you off on an extended, extemporaneous speech. The board is not usually seeking more information. The question is principally to offer you a last opportunity to present further qualifications or to indicate that you have nothing to add. So, if you feel that a significant qualification or characteristic has been overlooked, it is proper to point it out in a sentence or so. Do not compliment the board on the thoroughness of their examination – they have been sketchy, and you know it. If you wish, merely say, "No thank you, I have nothing further to add." This is a point where you can "talk yourself out" of a good impression or fail to present an important bit of information. Remember, *you close the interview yourself*.

The chairman will then say, "That is all, Mr. _____, thank you." Do not be startled; the interview is over, and quicker than you think. Thank him, gather your belongings and take your leave. Save your sigh of relief for the other side of the door.

How to put your best foot forward
Throughout this entire process, you may feel that the board individually and collectively is trying to pierce your defenses, seek out your hidden weaknesses and embarrass and confuse you. Actually, this is not true. They are obliged to make an appraisal of your qualifications for the job you are seeking, and they want to see you in your best light. Remember, they must interview all candidates and a non-cooperative candidate may become a failure in spite of their best efforts to bring out his qualifications. Here are 15 suggestions that will help you:

1) Be natural – Keep your attitude confident, not cocky
If you are not confident that you can do the job, do not expect the board to be. Do not apologize for your weaknesses, try to bring out your strong points. The board is interested in a positive, not negative, presentation. Cockiness will antagonize any board member and make him wonder if you are covering up a weakness by a false show of strength.

2) Get comfortable, but don't lounge or sprawl
Sit erectly but not stiffly. A careless posture may lead the board to conclude that you are careless in other things, or at least that you are not impressed by the importance of the occasion. Either conclusion is natural, even if incorrect. Do not fuss with your clothing, a pencil or an ashtray. Your hands may occasionally be useful to emphasize a point; do not let them become a point of distraction.

3) Do not wisecrack or make small talk
This is a serious situation, and your attitude should show that you consider it as such. Further, the time of the board is limited – they do not want to waste it, and neither should you.

4) Do not exaggerate your experience or abilities
In the first place, from information in the application or other interviews and sources, the board may know more about you than you think. Secondly, you probably will not get away with it. An experienced board is rather adept at spotting such a situation, so do not take the chance.

5) If you know a board member, do not make a point of it, yet do not hide it
Certainly you are not fooling him, and probably not the other members of the board. Do not try to take advantage of your acquaintanceship – it will probably do you little good.

6) Do not dominate the interview
Let the board do that. They will give you the clues – do not assume that you have to do all the talking. Realize that the board has a number of questions to ask you, and do not try to take up all the interview time by showing off your extensive knowledge of the answer to the first one.

7) Be attentive
You only have 20 minutes or so, and you should keep your attention at its sharpest throughout. When a member is addressing a problem or question to you, give him your undivided attention. Address your reply principally to him, but do not exclude the other board members.

8) Do not interrupt
A board member may be stating a problem for you to analyze. He will ask you a question when the time comes. Let him state the problem, and wait for the question.

9) Make sure you understand the question
Do not try to answer until you are sure what the question is. If it is not clear, restate it in your own words or ask the board member to clarify it for you. However, do not haggle about minor elements.

10) Reply promptly but not hastily
A common entry on oral board rating sheets is "candidate responded readily," or "candidate hesitated in replies." Respond as promptly and quickly as you can, but do not jump to a hasty, ill-considered answer.

11) Do not be peremptory in your answers
A brief answer is proper – but do not fire your answer back. That is a losing game from your point of view. The board member can probably ask questions much faster than you can answer them.

12) Do not try to create the answer you think the board member wants
He is interested in what kind of mind you have and how it works – not in playing games. Furthermore, he can usually spot this practice and will actually grade you down on it.

13) Do not switch sides in your reply merely to agree with a board member
Frequently, a member will take a contrary position merely to draw you out and to see if you are willing and able to defend your point of view. Do not start a debate, yet do not surrender a good position. If a position is worth taking, it is worth defending.

14) Do not be afraid to admit an error in judgment if you are shown to be wrong

The board knows that you are forced to reply without any opportunity for careful consideration. Your answer may be demonstrably wrong. If so, admit it and get on with the interview.

15) Do not dwell at length on your present job

The opening question may relate to your present assignment. Answer the question but do not go into an extended discussion. You are being examined for a *new* job, not your present one. As a matter of fact, try to phrase ALL your answers in terms of the job for which you are being examined.

Basis of Rating

Probably you will forget most of these "do's" and "don'ts" when you walk into the oral interview room. Even remembering them all will not ensure you a passing grade. Perhaps you did not have the qualifications in the first place. But remembering them will help you to put your best foot forward, without treading on the toes of the board members.

Rumor and popular opinion to the contrary notwithstanding, an oral board wants you to make the best appearance possible. They know you are under pressure – but they also want to see how you respond to it as a guide to what your reaction would be under the pressures of the job you seek. They will be influenced by the degree of poise you display, the personal traits you show and the manner in which you respond.

ABOUT THIS BOOK

This book contains tests divided into Examination Sections. Go through each test, answering every question in the margin. We have also attached a sample answer sheet at the back of the book that can be removed and used. At the end of each test look at the answer key and check your answers. On the ones you got wrong, look at the right answer choice and learn. Do not fill in the answers first. Do not memorize the questions and answers, but understand the answer and principles involved. On your test, the questions will likely be different from the samples. Questions are changed and new ones added. If you understand these past questions you should have success with any changes that arise. Tests may consist of several types of questions. We have additional books on each subject should more study be advisable or necessary for you. Finally, the more you study, the better prepared you will be. This book is intended to be the last thing you study before you walk into the examination room. Prior study of relevant texts is also recommended. NLC publishes some of these in our Fundamental Series. Knowledge and good sense are important factors in passing your exam. Good luck also helps. So now study this Passbook, absorb the material contained within and take that knowledge into the examination. Then do your best to pass that exam.

EXAMINATION SECTION

EXAMINATION SECTION
TEST 1

DIRECTIONS: Each question or incomplete statement is followed by several suggested answers or completions. Select the one that BEST answers the question or completes the statement. *PRINT THE LETTER OF THE CORRECT ANSWER IN THE SPACE AT THE RIGHT.*

Questions 1-6.

DIRECTIONS: Questions 1 through 6 are to be answered on the basis of the circuit diagram below. All switches are initially open.

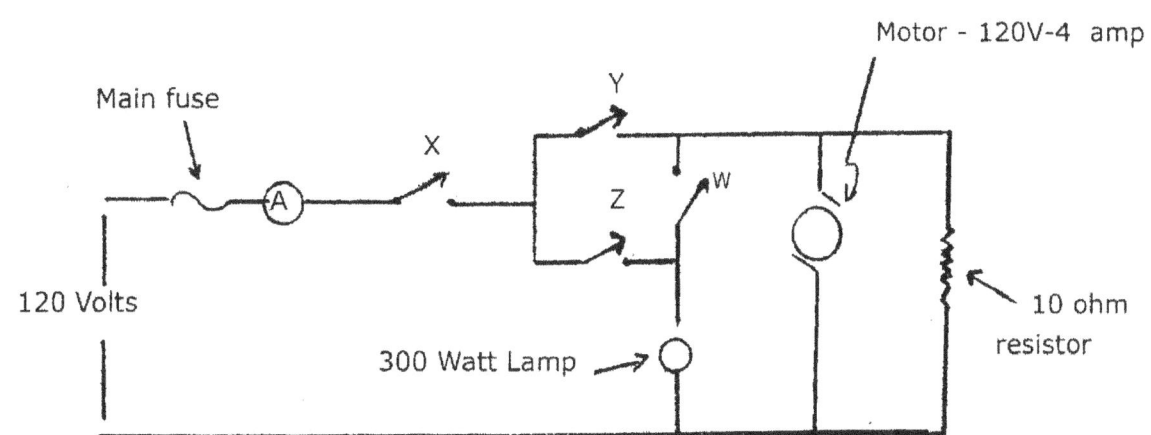

1. To light the 300 watt lamp, the following switches MUST be closed: 1.____
   A. X and Y B. Y and Z C. X and Z D. X and W

2. If all of the switches W, X, Y, and Z are closed, the following will happen: 2.____
   A. The lamp will light and the motor will rotate
   B. The lamp will light and the motor will not rotate
   C. The lamp will not light and the motor will not rotate
   D. A short circuit will occur and the main fuse will blow

3. With 120 volts applied across the 10 ohm resistor, the current drawn by the resistor is ____ amp(s). 3.____
   A. 1/12 B. 1.2 C. 12 D. 1200

4. With 120 volts applied to the 10 ohm resistor, the power used by the resistor is ____ kw. 4.____
   A. 1.44 B. 1.2 C. .144 D. .12

5. The current drawn by the 300 watt lamp when lighted should be APPROXIMATELY ____ amps. 5.____
   A. 2.5 B. 3.6 C. 25 D. 36

1

6. In the circuit shown, the symbol A is used to indicate a (n)

   A. ammeter
   B. *and* circuit
   C. voltmeter
   D. wattmeter

7. Of the following materials, the BEST conductor of electricity is

   A. iron   B. copper   C. aluminum   D. glass

8. The sum of 6'6", 5'9", and 2' 1 1/2" is

   A. 13'4 1/2"   B. 13'6 1/2"   C. 14'4 1/2"   D. 14'6 1/2"

9.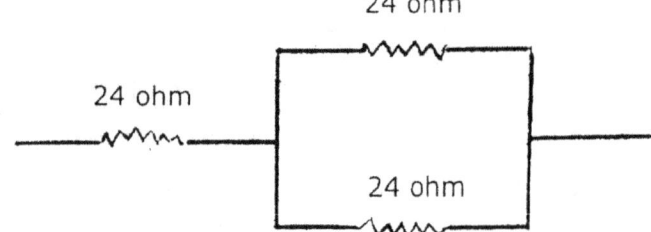

   The equivalent resistance of the three resistors shown in the sketch above is _____ ohms.

   A. 8   B. 24   C. 36   D. 72

10.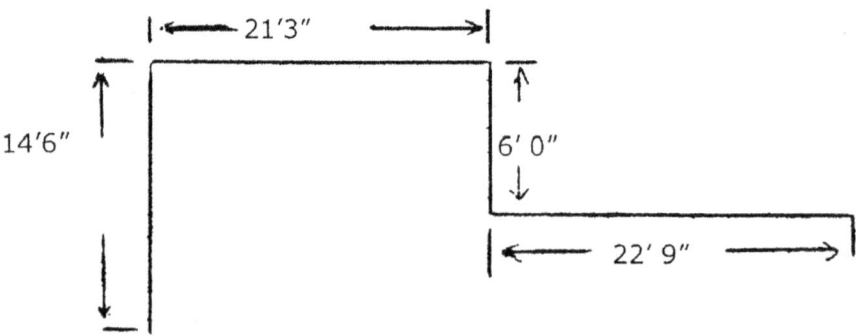

    The TOTAL length of electrical conduit that must be run along the path shown on the diagram above is

    A. 63'8"   B. 64'6"   C. 65'6"   D. 66'8"

11. Of the following electrical devices, the one that is NOT normally used in direct current electrical circuits is a (n)

    A. circuit breaker
    B. double-pole switch
    C. transformer
    D. inverter

12. The number of 120-volt light bulbs that should NORMALLY be connected in series across a 600-volt electric line is

    A. 1   B. 2   C. 3   D. 5

13. Of the following motors, the one that does NOT have any brushes is the _____ motor. 13._____

    A. d.c. shunt B. d.c. series
    C. squirrel cage induction D. compound

14. Of the following materials, the one that is COMMONLY used as an electric heating element in an electric heater is 14._____

    A. zinc B. brass
    C. terne plate D. nichrome

Questions 15-25.

DIRECTIONS: Questions 15 through 25 are to be answered on the basis of the instruments listed below. Each instrument is listed with an identifying number in front of it.

  1 - Hygrometer   9 - Vernier caliper
  2 - Ammeter   10 - Wire gage
  3 - Voltmeter   11 - 6-foot folding rule
  4 - Wattmeter   12 - Architect's scale
  5 - Megger   13 - Planimeter
  6 - Oscilloscope   14 - Engineer's scale
  7 - Frequency meter 15 - Ohmmeter
  8 - Micrometer

15. The instrument that should be used to accurately measure the resistance of a 4,700 ohm resistor is Number 15._____

    A. 3 B. 4 C. 7 D. 15

16. To measure the current in an electrical circuit, the instrument that should be used is Number 16._____

    A. 2 B. 7 C. 8 D. 15

17. To measure the insulation resistance of a rubber-covered electrical cable, the instrument that should be used is Number 17._____

    A. 4 B. 5 C. 8 D. 15

18. An AC motor is hooked up to a power distribution box. 18._____
    In order to check the voltage at the motor terminals, the instrument that should be used is Number

    A. 2 B. 3 C. 4 D. 7

19. To measure the shaft diameter of a motor accurately to one-thousandth of an inch, the instrument that should be used is Number 19._____

    A. 8 B. 10 C. 11 D. 14

20. The instrument that should be used to determine whether 25 Hz. or 60 Hz. is present in an electrical circuit is Number 20._____

    A. 4 B. 5 C. 7 D. 8

21. Of the following, the PROPER instrument to use to determine the diameter of the conductor of a piece of electrical hook-up wire is Number

    A. 10   B. 11   C. 12   D. 14

22. The amount of electrical power being used in a balanced three-phase circuit should be measured with Number

    A. 2   B. 3   C. 4   D. 5

23. The electrical wave form at a given point in an electronic circuit can be observed with Number

    A. 2   B. 3   C. 6   D. 7

24. The PROPER instrument to use for measuring the width of a door is Number

    A. 11   B. 12   C. 13   D. 14

25. A one-inch hole with a tolerance of plus or minus three-thousandths is reamed in a steel block.
    The PROPER instrument to use to accurately check the diameter of the hole is Number

    A. 8   B. 9   C. 11   D. 14

KEY (CORRECT ANSWERS)

1. C
2. A
3. C
4. A
5. A

6. A
7. B
8. C
9. C
10. B

11. C
12. D
13. C
14. D
15. D

16. A
17. B
18. B
19. A
20. C

21. A
22. C
23. C
24. A
25. B

TEST 2

DIRECTIONS: Each question or incomplete statement is followed by several suggested answers or completions. Select the one that BEST answers the question or completes the statement. *PRINT THE LETTER OF THE CORRECT ANSWER IN THE SPACE AT THE RIGHT.*

1. The number of conductors required to connect a 3-phase delta connected heater bank to an electric power panel board is

    A. 2 B. 3 C. 4 D. 5

2. Of the following, the wire size that is MOST commonly used for branch lighting circuits in homes is _____ A.W.G.

    A. #12 B. #8 C. #6 D. #4

3. When installing electrical circuits, the tool that should be used to pull wire through a conduit is a

    A. mandrel
    B. snake
    C. rod
    D. pulling iron

4. Of the following AC voltages, the LOWEST voltage that a neon test lamp can detect is _____ volts.

    A. 6 B. 12 C. 80 D. 120

5. Of the following, the BEST procedure to use when storing tools that are subject to rusting is to

    A. apply a thin coating of soap onto the tools
    B. apply a light coating of oil to the tools
    C. wrap the tools in clean cheesecloth
    D. place the tools in a covered container

6. If a 3 1/2 inch long nail is required to nail wood framing members together, the nail size to use should be

    A. 2d B. 4d C. 16d D. 60d

7. Of the four motors listed below, the one that can operate only on alternating current is a(n) _____ motor.

    A. series
    B. shunt
    C. compound
    D. induction

8. The sum of 1/3 + 2/5 + 5/6 is

    A. 1 17/30 B. 1 3/5 C. 1 15/24 D. 1 5/6

9. Of the following instruments, the one that should be used to measure the state of charge of a lead-acid storage battery is a(n)

    A. ammeter
    B. ohmmeter
    C. hydrometer
    D. thermometer

10. If three 1 1/2 volt dry cell batteries are wired in series, the TOTAL voltage provided by the three batteries is _____ volts. 10._____

    A. 1.5 B. 3 C. 4.5 D. 6.0

11. Taking into account time and one-half payment for time over 40 hours of work, the gross pay of an employee who works 43 hours in a week at a rate of pay of $10.68 per hour is 11._____

    A. $427.20 B. $459.24 C. $475.26 D. $491.28

12. The sum of 0.365 + 3.941 + 10.676 + 0.784 is 12._____

    A. 13.766 B. 15.666 C. 15.756 D. 15.766

13. In order to transmit mechanical power between two rotating shafts at right angles to each other, two gears are used. Of the following, the type of gears that should be used are _____ gears. 13._____

    A. herringbone B. spur
    C. bevel D. rack and pinion

14. To properly ground the service electrical equipment in a building, a ground connection should be made to _____ the building. 14._____

    A. the waste or soil line leaving
    B. the vent line going to the exterior of
    C. any steel beam in
    D. the cold water line entering

15. The area of the triangle shown at the right is _____ square inches. 15._____
    A. 120
    B. 240
    C. 360
    D. 480

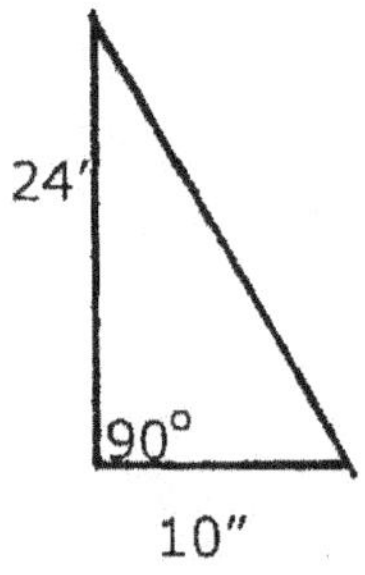

Questions 16-25.

DIRECTIONS: Questions 16 through 25 are to be answered on the basis of the tools shown on the next page. The tools are not shown to scale. Each tool is shown with an identifying number alongside it.

3 (#2)

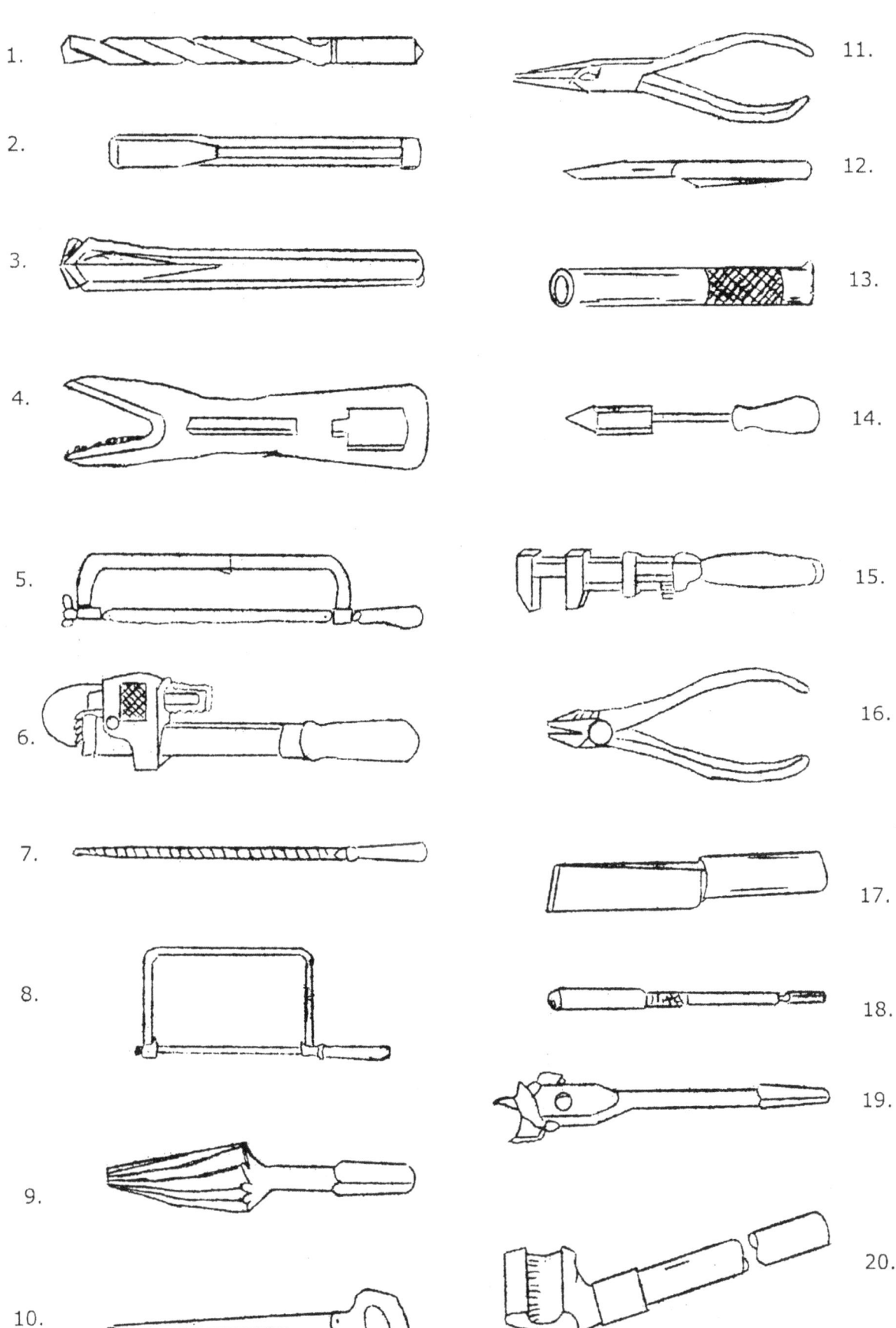

16. The tool that should be used for cutting thin wall steel conduit is Number

    A. 5   B. 8   C. 10   D. 16

17. The tool that should be used for cutting a 1 7/8 inch diameter hole in a wood joist is Number

    A. 3   B. 9   C. 14   D. 19

18. The tool that should be used for soldering splices in electrical wire is Number

    A. 3   B. 7   C. 13   D. 14

19. After cutting off a piece of 3/4 inch diameter electrical conduit, the tool that should be used for removing a burr from the inside of the conduit is Number

    A. 9   B. 11   C. 12   D. 14

20. The tool that should be used for turning a coupling onto a threaded conduit is Number

    A. 6   B. 11   C. 15   D. 16

21. The tool that should be used for cutting wood lathing in plaster walls is Number

    A. 5   B. 7   C. 10   D. 12

22. The tool that should be used for drilling a 3/8 inch diameter hole in a steel beam is Number

    A. 1   B. 2   C. 3   D. 9

23. Of the following, the BEST tool to use for stripping insulation from electrical hook-up wire is Number

    A. 11   B. 12   C. 15   D. 20

24. The tool that should be used for bending an electrical wire around a terminal post is Number

    A. 4   B. 11   C. 15   D. 16

25. The tool that should be used for cutting electrical hookup wire is Number

    A. 5   B. 12   C. 16   D. 17

KEY (CORRECT ANSWERS)

1. B
2. A
3. B
4. C
5. B

6. C
7. D
8. A
9. C
10. C

11. C
12. D
13. C
14. D
15. A

16. A
17. D
18. D
19. A
20. A

21. C
22. A
23. B
24. B
25. C

TEST 3

DIRECTIONS: Each question or incomplete statement is followed by several suggested answers or completions. Select the one that BEST answers the question or completes the statement. *PRINT THE LETTER OF THE CORRECT ANSWER IN THE SPACE AT THE RIGHT.*

1. An electric circuit has current flowing through it. The panel board switch feeding the circuit is opened, causing arcing across the switch contacts.
   Generally, this arcing is caused by

   A. a lack of energy storage in the circuit
   B. electrical energy stored by a capacitor
   C. electrical energy stored by a resistor
   D. magnetic energy induced by an inductance

   1.____

2. MOST filter capacitors in radios have a capacity rating given in

   A. microvolts   B. milliamps
   C. millihenries   D. microfarads

   2.____

3. Of the following, the electrical wire size that is COMMONLY used for telephone circuits is _____ A.W.G.

   A. #6   B. #10   C. #12   D. #22

   3.____

Questions 4-9.

DIRECTIONS: Questions 4 through 9 are to be answered on the basis of the electrical circuit diagram shown below, where letters are used to identify various circuit components.

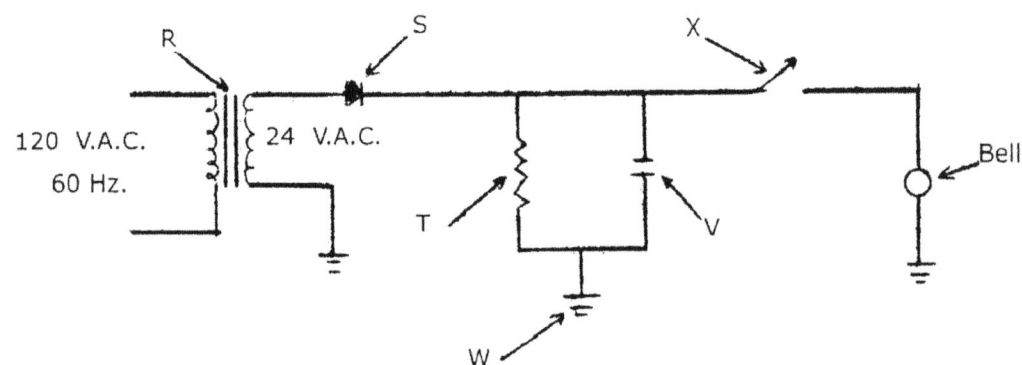

4. The device indicated by the letter R is a

   A. capacitor   B. converter
   C. resistor   D. transformer

   4.____

5. The device indicated by the letter S is a

   A. transistor   B. diode
   C. thermistor   D. directional relay

   5.____

6. The devices indicated by the letters T and V are used together to _____ components of the secondary current.

    A. reduce the AC
    B. reduce the DC
    C. transform the AC
    D. invert the AC

7. The letter W points to a standard electrical symbol for a

    A. wire
    B. ground
    C. terminal
    D. lightning arrestor

8. Closing switch X will apply the following type of voltage to the bell:

    A. 60 Hz. AC
    B. DC
    C. pulsating AC
    D. 120 Hz. AC

9. The circuit shown contains a _____ rectifier.

    A. mercury-arc
    B. full-wave
    C. bridge
    D. half-wave

10. A bolt specified as 1/4-28 means the following:
    The

    A. bolt is 1/4 inch in diameter and has 28 threads per inch
    B. bolt is 1/4 inch in diameter and is 2.8 inches long
    C. bolt is 1/4 inch long and has 28 threads
    D. threaded portion of the bolt is 1/4 inch long and has 28 threads per inch

11. When cutting 0.045-inch thickness sheet metal, it is BEST to use a hacksaw blade that has _____ teeth per inch.

    A. 7
    B. 12
    C. 18
    D. 32

12. To accurately tighten a bolt to 28 foot-pounds, it is BEST to use a(n) _____ wrench.

    A. pipe
    B. open end
    C. box
    D. torque

13. When bending a 2-inch diameter conduit, the CORRECT tool to use is a

    A. hickey
    B. pipe wrench
    C. hydraulic bender
    D. stock and die

14. When soldering two #20 A.W.G. copper wires together to form a splice, the solder that SHOULD be used is _____ solder.

    A. acid-core
    B. solid-core
    C. rosin-core
    D. liquid

15. A bathroom heating unit draws 10 amperes at 115 volts.
    The hot resistance of the heating unit should be _____ ohms.

    A. .08
    B. 8
    C. 11.5
    D. 1150

16. Of the following materials, the one that is NOT suitable as an electrical insulator is

    A. glass
    B. mica
    C. rubber
    D. platinum

17. An air conditioning unit is rated at 1000 watts. The unit is run for 10 hours per day, five days per week.
If the cost for electrical energy is 5 cents per kilowatt-hour, the weekly cost for electricity should be

    A. 25¢   B. 50¢   C. $2.50   D. $25.00

17.____

18. If a fuse is protecting the circuit of a 15 ohm electric heater and it is designed to blow out at a current exceeding 10 amperes, the MAXIMUM voltage from among the following that should be applied across the terminals of the heater is _____ volts.

    A. 110   B. 120   C. 160   D. 600

18.____

19. Before opening a pneumatic hose connection, it is important to remove pressure from the hose line PRIMARILY to avoid

    A. losing air
    B. personal injury
    C. damage to the hose connection
    D. a build-up of pressure in the air compressor

19.____

20. If the scale on a shop drawing is 1/4 inch to the foot, then a part which measures 3 3/8 inches long on the drawing has an ACTUAL length of _____ feet _____ inches.

    A. 12; 6   B. 13; 6   C. 13; 9   D. 14; 9

20.____

21. The function that is USUALLY performed by a motor controller is to

    A. start and stop a motor
    B. protect a motor from a short circuit
    C. prevent bearing failure of a motor
    D. control the brush wear in a motor

21.____

22. Of the following galvanized sheet metal electrical outlet boxes, the one that is NOT a commonly used size is the _____ box.

    A. 4" square   B. 4" octagonal
    C. 4" x 2 1/8"   D. 4" x 1"

22.____

23. When soldering a transistor into a circuit, it is MOST important to protect the transistor from

    A. the application of an excess of rosin flux
    B. excessive heat
    C. the application of an excess of solder
    D. too much pressure

23.____

24. When installing BX type cable, it is important to protect the wires in the cable from the cut ends of the armored sheath.
The APPROVED method of providing this protection is to

    A. use a fiber or plastic insulating bushing
    B. file the cut ends of the sheath smooth
    C. use a connector where the cable enters a junction box
    D. tie the wires into an Underwriter's knot

24.____

25. While lifting a heavy piece of equipment off the floor, a person should NOT

    A. twist his body
    B. grasp it firmly
    C. maintain a solid footing on the ground
    D. bend his knees

26. It is important that metal cabinets and panels that house electrical equipment should be grounded PRIMARILY in order to

    A. prevent short circuits from occurring
    B. keep all circuits at ground potential
    C. minimize shock hazards
    D. reduce the effects of electrolytic corrosion

27. A foreman explains a technical procedure to a new employee. If the employee does not understand the instructions he has received, it would be BEST if he were to

    A. follow the procedure as best he could
    B. ask the foreman to explain it to him again
    C. avoid following the procedure
    D. ask the foreman to give him other work

28. Of the following, the BEST connectors to use when mounting an electrical panel box directly onto a concrete wall are

    A. threaded studs   B. machine screws
    C. lag screws   D. expansion bolts

29. Of the following, the BEST instrument to use to measure the small gap between relay contacts is

    A. a micrometer   B. a feeler gage
    C. inside calipers   D. a plug gage

30. A POSSIBLE result of mounting a 40 ampere fuse in a fuse box for a circuit requiring a 20 ampere fuse is that the 40 ampere fuse may

    A. provide twice as much protection to the circuit from overloads
    B. blow more easily than the smaller fuse due to an overload
    C. cause serious damage to the circuit from an overload
    D. reduce power consumption in the circuit

KEY (CORRECT ANSWERS)

1.	D	16.	D
2.	D	17.	C
3.	D	18.	B
4.	D	19.	B
5.	B	20.	B
6.	A	21.	A
7.	B	22.	D
8.	B	23.	B
9.	D	24.	A
10.	A	25.	A
11.	D	26.	C
12.	D	27.	B
13.	C	28.	D
14.	C	29.	B
15.	C	30.	C

EXAMINATION SECTION
TEST 1

DIRECTIONS: Each question or incomplete statement is followed by several suggested answers or completions. Select the one that *BEST* answers the question or completes the statement. *PRINT THE LETTER OF THE CORRECT ANSWER IN THE SPACE AT THE RIGHT.*

1. Asbestos was used as a wire covering mainly for protection against 1.____
   A. humidity B. vibration C. corrosion D. heat

2. A wattmeter is used for making a direct measurement of 2.____
   A. current B. voltage C. power D. resistance

3. The number of connection points to a two-pole, double-throw knife switch is 3.____
   A. 2 B. 4 C. 6 D. 8

4. Wires are pulled through conduit with the aid of 4.____
   A. a hickey B. an extension bit
   C. a snake D. a nipple

5. To smooth out the ripples present in rectified a.c., the device commonly used is a 5.____
   A. filter B. relay C. spark gap D. booster

6. A tachometer is used for measuring 6.____
   A. r.p.m. B. torque
   C. power factor D. specific gravity

7. Rubber insulation deteriorates most rapidly when in contact with 7.____
   A. water B. oil C. lead D. aluminum

8. The microfarad is a unit of measurement used for condenser 8.____
   A. ohmic resistance B. power loss
   C. leakage current D. capacity

9. A "megger" is an electrical instrument used to measure 9.____
   A. current B. resistance
   C. voltage D. wattage

10. When a run of conduit would require many right angle bends, it is necessary to install pull boxes because 10.____
    A. conduit cannot be bent
    B. otherwise injury to the wires may result during installation
    C. conduit comes in fixed lengths
    D. the conduit requires support

11. The metal frames of some electrical units are grounded mainly to

    A. eliminate short-circuits
    B. save insulating material
    C. protect against shock
    D. prevent overloading

12. A motor which can be operated only from an a.c. power source is

    A. a shunt motor   B. a series motor
    C. a compound motor   D. an induction motor

13. Of the following, the poorest conductor of electricity is

    A. mercury   B. sulphuric acid
    C. distilled water   D. salt water

14. The insulation provided between commutator bars on a d.c. motor is generally

    A. mica   B. lucite   C. porcelain   D. transite

15. Nichrome wire should be most suitable for use in

    A. a transformer   B. a motor
    C. an incandescent lamp   D. a heating element

16. Electrical outlet boxes do not have to be drilled for the entrance of conduit into the boxes if they are provided with

    A. bushings   B. knockouts   C. hickeys   D. couplings

17. The minimum number of field windings in a compound motor is

    A. 1   B. 2   C. 3   D. 4

18. The motor most likely to reach a dangerous speed if operated at normal voltage and no load is a

    A. shunt motor   B. series motor
    C. compound motor   D. synchronous motor

19. If three 6-volt batteries are connected in parallel, the resultant voltage will be

    A. 18 volts   B. 9 volts   C. 6 volts   D. 2 volts

20. If an incandescent lamp is operated at a voltage below its rated voltage then it

    A. will operate more efficiently
    B. will have a longer life
    C. will take more power
    D. is more likely to fail by arcing

21. Four resistors, having respective current ratings of 1, 2, 3 and 4 amperes, are connected in series. If the resistors are not to be overloaded, the maximum current permissable in this circuit is

    A. 1 ampere   B. 2.5 amperes
    C. 4 amperes   D. 10 amperes

22. Conduit is reamed mainly to 22.____

    A. protect the wires against sharp edges
    B. make threading easier
    C. increase its electrical conductivity
    D. improve its appearance

23. Two 25-watt, 120-volt lamps are connected in parallel to a 120-volt source. The two lamps will take a total of 23.____

    A. 12.5 watts   B. 25 watts
    C. 50 watts   D. 100 watts

24. An advantage of the mercury arc rectifiers when compared to rotary converters is that the mercury arc rectifiers 24.____

    A. are relatively quiet
    B. eliminate the use of transformers
    C. operate at lower voltage
    D. operate for shorter periods

25. A bushing is usually provided on the end of a conduit running into a panel box. An important function of the bushing is to 25.____

    A. insulate the conduit from the panel box
    B. support the panel box
    C. separate one conduit from another
    D. prevent injury to the wires

26. An alternator is 26.____

    A. an a.c. generator
    B. a ground detector device
    C. a choke coil
    D. a frequency meter

27. The best immediate first-aid treatment for a scraped knee is to 27.____

    A. apply plain vaseline
    B. use a knee splint
    C. apply heat
    D. wash it with soap and water

Questions 28 - 34.

Questions 28 through 34 are based on the Signal System Emergency Power Supply Information given below. Read this information carefully before answering these questions.

SIGNAL SYSTEM EMERGENCY POWER SUPPLY INFORMATION

The signal mains operate on 115 volts a.c. and are fed from either a normal power supply or an emergency power supply. When the normal power supply goes below 90 volts, a transfer switch automatically switches the signal mains to the emergency power. With normal feed, the transfer switch is held in the normal or energized position. When the normal power supply falls, the transfer switch changes to the emergency supply by means of gravity and a control spring. The operation of the transfer switch is controlled by means of a potential relay which opens on less than 90 volts. Once the transfer switch has changed to the emergency side, it can only be reset to the normal side by first closing the potential relay by hand. If the normal supply is satisfactory, this relay will remain closed. Then by pushing a reset button, the transfer switch will swing to the normal side and remain-closed through its retaining circuit. A special push button is provided for checking the transfer switch for proper operation.

28. The transfer switch will automatically connect the signal mains to emergency power when the normal power supply voltage is

    A. 120 volts   B. 115 volts   C. 95 volts   D. 85 volts

29. The FIRST step in resetting the transfer switch to the normal side is to

    A. open the potential relay
    B. push the reset button
    C. operate the special button
    D. close the potential relay

30. The special push button is provided for

    A. checking the operation of the transfer switch
    B. disconnecting the emergency supply
    C. automatically closing the potential relay
    D. resetting the control spring

31. The reset button is used to

    A. swing the transfer switch to the normal side
    B. swing the transfer switch to the emergency side
    C. energize the potential relay
    D. de-energize the potential relay

32. The signal mains receive their power through the

    A. potential relay
    B. transfer switch
    C. reset button
    D. special push button

33. When the emergency power is feeding the signal mains, then the

    A. transfer switch is automatically energized
    B. potential relay automatically goes to the closed position
    C. transfer switch is in the de-energized position
    D. special push button must be pressed to restore the normal power supply

34. The transfer switch is held in the emergency supply position by

    A. a retaining circuit
    B. a special push button
    C. gravity and a control spring
    D. a reset button

35. To reduce the pitting of relay contacts which make and break frequently, the unit generally connected across them is a

    A. transistor
    B. spark gap
    C. condenser
    D. switch

36. As compared to a solid conductor, a stranded conductor of the same diameter

    A. has greater flexibility
    B. requires less insulation
    C. has greater resistance to corrosion
    D. does not require soldered connections

37. The electrolyte in a lead storage battery is

    A. sodium bicarbonate   B. sulphuric acid
    C. muriatic acid   D. ammonia

38. Twisted pair wire is desirable for telephone circuits mainly because it

    A. is less likely to pick up electrical interference
    B. can be run in long stretches without any support
    C. can carry heavy currents
    D. can withstand high voltage

39. In the subway, heavy copper bonds are connected across the joints of the track rails. With the bonds installed, a voltage drop measurement is taken across the track rail joint. This test would be used mainly to determine the bond

    A. temperature   B. electrical resistance
    C. breakdown voltage   D. leakage current

40. In a polarized electric cord plug, the contact blades of the plug are

    A. magnetized
    B. of different color
    C. parallel to each other
    D. perpendicular to each other

41. A capacity rating expressed in ampere-hours is commonly used for

    A. insulators   B. storage batteries
    C. switches   D. inductances

42. The number of ordinary flashlight cells which must be connected together to obtain 6 volts is

    A. 1   B. 2   C. 3   D. 4

43. A bank of five 120-volt lamps connected in series is used for test purposes in the subway. This test bank would be best utilized in checking a circuit having

    A. 120 volts d.c.   B. 120 volts a.c.
    C. 24 volts   D. 600 volts

44. A step-up transformer is used to step up

    A. voltage   B. current   C. power   D. frequency

45. A photoelectric cell is a device for changing

    A. light into electricity
    B. electricity into light
    C. electricity into heat
    D. sound into electricity

46. Decreasing the length of a wire conductor will

    A. increase the current carrying capacity
    B. decrease the current carrying capacity
    C. decrease the resistance
    D. increase the resistance

47. The proper tool to use in making a hole through a transite panel is

    A. a star drill   B. a countersink
    C. a twist drill   D. an auger

48. Copper is a preferred metal in the construction of large knife switches because it is

    A. soft   B. flexible
    C. a good conductor   D. light in weight

49. The process of removing the insulation from a wire is called

    A. sweating   B. skinning
    C. tinning   D. braiding

50. The electric lamp which is used for providing heat is

    A. a sodium vapor lamp   B. a mercury vapor lamp
    C. a neon lamp   D. an infra-red lamp

KEY (CORRECT ANSWERS)

1. D	11. C	21. A	31. A	41. B
2. C	12. D	22. A	32. B	42. D
3. C	13. C	23. C	33. C	43. D
4. C	14. A	24. A	34. C	44. A
5. A	15. D	25. D	35. C	45. A
6. A	16. B	26. A	36. A	46. C
7. B	17. B	27. D	37. B	47. C
8. D	18. B	28. D	38. A	48. C
9. B	19. C	29. D	39. B	49. B
10. B	20. B	30. A	40. D	50. D

TEST 2

DIRECTIONS: Each question or incomplete statement is followed by several suggested answers or completions. Select the one that BEST answers the question or completes the statement. *PRINT THE LETTER OF THE CORRECT ANSWER IN THE SPACE AT THE RIGHT.*

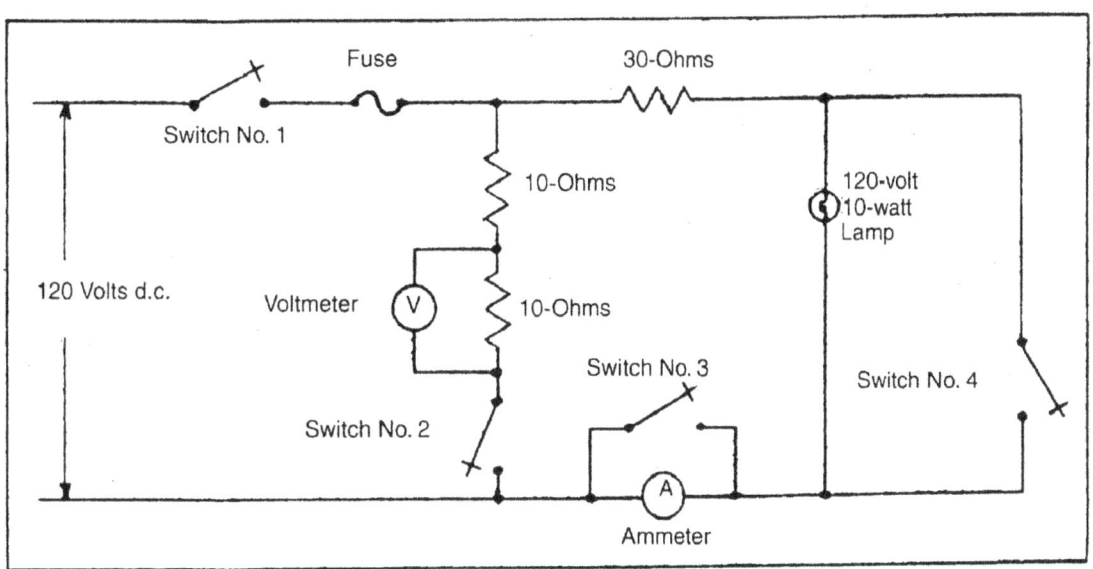

Questions 1-7

Questions 1 through 7 are based on the above wiring diagram. Refer to this diagram when answering these questions.

1. Starting with all switches open, then to light the lamp it is necessary to close switch   1._____

    A. No. 1   B. No. 2   C. No. 3   D. No. 4

2. Closing one of the four switches will prevent the lamp from being lighted. This switch is   2._____

    A. No. 1   B. No. 2   C. No. 3   D. No. 4

3. The two switches which must be in the closed position to obtain a reading on the voltmeter are   3._____

    A. No. 1 and No. 4   B. No. 2 and No. 3
    C. No. 3 and No. 4   D. No.1 and No. 2

4. To obtain a reading on the ammeter it is necessary to have   4._____

    A. switch No. 2 open
    B. switch No. 4 closed
    C. switch No. 3 closed and switch No. 1 open
    D. switch No. 3 open and switch No. 1 closed

21

5. When current is flowing through the 10-ohm resistors, the voltmeter reading will be   5.____
   A. 100 volts   B. 60 volts   C. 40 volts   D. 24 volts

6. In this circuit the ammeter should have a scale range of at least zero to   6.____
   A. 1 ampere   B. 2 amperes   C. 3 amperes   D. 4 amperes

7. With the switches set for this circuit to take maximum current from the line, then the current through the fuse will be approximately   7.____
   A. 1 ampere   B. 2 amperes   C. 4 amperes   D. 10 amperes

8. The abbreviations I.D. and O.D. used in describing conduit directly refer to its   8.____
   A. diameter   B. length   C. conductivity   D. weight

9. To cut off a piece of #0000 insulated copper cable it is best to use   9.____
   A. a hacksaw   B. side-cutting pliers
   C. an electrician's knife   D. light nippers

10. Conduit is galvanized in order to   10.____
    A. improve electrical conductivity   B. protect it from corrosion
    C. obtain a smooth surface   D. insulate it

11. The best material for an electrical contact finger subjected to constant bending is   11.____
    A. brass   B. aluminum
    C. tin   D. phosphor bronze

12. One disadvantage of porcelain as an insulator is that it is   12.____
    A. only good for low voltage
    B. not satisfactory on a-c circuits
    C. a brittle material
    D. easily compressed

13. To vary the speed of a d-c motor-generator set, it would be necessary to   13.____
    A. use a rheostat in the generator field
    B. use a voltage regulator on the generator output
    C. use a rheostat in the motor field
    D. shift the brushes on the generator

14. The ordinary telephone transmitter contains granules of   14.____
    A. sulphur   B. carbon   C. borax   D. lucite

15. A stubby screwdriver is especially designed for turning screws   15.____
    A. having a damaged screw slot
    B. which are jammed tight
    C. with stripped threads
    D. inaccessible to a longer screwdriver

16. It is important to make certain a ladle does not contain water before using it to scoop up molten solder since the water may 16.____

    A. cause serious personal injury
    B. prevent the solder from sticking
    C. cool the solder
    D. dilute the solder

17. Steel helmets give workers the most protection from 17.____

    A. eye injuries
    B. falling objects
    C. fire
    D. electric shock

18. A slight coating of rust on small tools is best removed by 18.____

    A. applying a heavy coat of vaseline
    B. rubbing with kerosene and fine steel wool
    C. scraping with a sharp knife
    D. rubbing with a dry cloth

19. In the case of an auto-transformer, it is *INCORRECT* to say that 19.____

    A. the primary is insulated from the secondary
    B. a magnetic core is used
    C. a.c. is required
    D. it can be used for power purposes

20. The number 6-32 for a machine screw specifies the diameter and the 20.____

    A. length
    B. the number of threads per inch
    C. type of head
    D. hardness

21. It is undesirable to allow a soldering iron to overheat since this would cause 21.____

    A. softening of the copper tip
    B. hardening of the copper tip
    C. the soldering fumes to become poisonous
    D. damage to the tinned surface of the tip

22. To measure the small gap between relay contacts, it would be best to use a 22.____

    A. vernier caliper
    B. depth gage
    C. feeler gage
    D. micrometer

23. Acid is not a desirable flux to use in soldering small connections mainly because it 23.____

    A. is corrosive
    B. is expensive
    C. requires skill in handling
    D. requires a very hot iron

24. It is good practice to use standard electrician's pliers to

    A. tighten nuts
    B. remove insulation from a wire
    C. cut BX sheath
    D. shorten a wood screw

25. Three resistors having respective resistances of 12 ohms, 5 ohms, and 1 ohm are connected in parallel. The combined resistance will be

    A. 18 ohms
    B. 6 ohms
    C. 4 ohms
    D. less than 1 ohm

26. The star drill is a multiple-pointed chisel used for drilling

    A. brass
    B. stone and concrete
    C. wood
    D. aluminum

27. A screwdriver in good condition should have a blade whose bottom edge is

    A. rounded
    B. knife-sharp
    C. chisel-shaped
    D. flat

28. From the standpoint of management, the most desirable characteristic in a newly appointed helper would be

    A. the lack of outside personal interests
    B. the ability to keep to himself and away from the other employees
    C. the ability to satisfactorily perform his assigned duties
    D. eagerness to ask questions about all phases of the work

29. To provide transit employees with quick assistance in the case of minor injuries it would be most logical to

    A. instruct the employees in first-aid techniques
    B. provide each employee with a first-aid kit
    C. have one centrally located medical office for the transit system
    D. equip all employees with walkie-talkie devices

30. One result of corrosion of an electrical connection is that

    A. its resistance increases
    B. its resistance decreases
    C. its temperature drops
    D. the current in the circuit increases

31. Subway cars are equipped with storage batteries. These batteries are LEAST likely to be used to supply power to the car

    A. traction motors
    B. emergency lights
    C. public address system
    D. motorman-conductor communication system

32. The size of a screwdriver is defined by the

   A. length of the handle
   B. thickness of the blade
   C. length of the blade
   D. diameter of the handle

33. A newly appointed helper would be expected to do his work in the manner prescribed by his foreman because

   A. it insures discipline
   B. good results are more certain with less supervision
   C. no other method would work
   D. it permits speed-up

34. When a soldered splice is covered with both rubber and friction tape, the main function of the friction tape is to

   A. provide extra electrical insulation
   B. protect the rubber tape
   C. make the splice water-tight
   D. increase the mechanical strength of the splice

35. Powdered graphite is a good

   A. lubricant   B. abrasive   C. adhesive   D. insulator

36. A zero adjusting screw will be found on most

   A. overload relays
   B. lightning arrestors
   C. voltmeters
   D. switches

37. Lock nuts are frequently used in making electrical connections on terminal boards. The purpose of the lock-nuts is to

   A. keep the connections from loosening through vibration
   B. prevent unauthorized personnel from tampering with the connections
   C. eliminate the use of flat washers
   D. increase the contact area at the connection point

38. The abbreviation D.P.D.T. used in electrical work describes a type of

   A. switch   B. motor   C. fuse   D. generator

39. A wire has a resistance of 2 ohms per 1000 feet. A piece of this wire 1500 feet long will have a resistance of

   A. 1 ohm   B. 1.5 ohms   C. 2.5 ohms   D. 3 ohms

40. The dielectric strength of the oil used in an oil filled transformer is a direct measure of the oil's

   A. viscosity
   B. weight
   C. breakdown voltage
   D. current carrying capacity

41. The power fed to a mercury arc rectifier would probably come from

    A. a rotary converter
    B. a d.c. generator
    C. an a.c. source
    D. a battery

42. The ordinary plug fuse has

    A. knife blade contacts
    B. screw base contacts
    C. ferrule contacts
    D. jack contacts

43. When using a hacksaw, it is good practice to

    A. tighten the blade in the frame by using pliers on the wing nut
    B. use heavy pressure on both the forward and return strokes
    C. slow the speed of cutting when the piece is almost cut through
    D. use very short, very rapid strokes

44. A new helper is told by an experienced helper that he is not doing a particular job properly. The best reason for the new helper to give this advice due consideration is that the other helper

    A. has the authority to enforce his advice
    B. has more experience on the job
    C. will be resentful if his advice is not taken
    D. will not help the new man again if his advice is not taken

45. The main purpose of the oil in an oil circuit breaker is to

    A. quench the arc
    B. lubricate the moving parts
    C. prevent corrosion
    D. absorb moisture

46. A piece of electrical equipment which does NOT require a magnetic field for its operation is

    A. a motor
    B. a generator
    C. a transformer
    D. an electrostatic voltmeter

47. The rating term "20-watts, 500-ohm" would generally be applied to a

    A. resistor
    B. condenser
    C. switch
    D. circuit breaker

48. The core of an electro-magnet is usually made of

    A. lead   B. iron   C. brass   D. bakelite

49. The A.W.G. size is used in specifying

    A. wires   B. condensers   C. switches   D. fuses

50. The metal which is preferred for use in relay contacts is

    A. brass   B. tin   C. silver   D. aluminum

KEY (CORRECT ANSWERS)

1. A	11. D	21. D	31. A	41. C
2. D	12. C	22. C	32. C	42. B
3. D	13. C	23. A	33. B	43. C
4. B	14. B	24. B	34. B	44. B
5. D	15. D	25. D	35. A	45. A
6. D	16. A	26. B	36. C	46. D
7. D	17. B	27. D	37. A	47. A
8. A	18. B	28. C	38. A	48. B
9. A	19. A	29. A	39. D	49. A
10. B	20. B	30. A	40. C	50. C

EXAMINATION SECTION
TEST 1

DIRECTIONS: Each question or incomplete statement is followed by several suggested answers or completions. Select the one that BEST answers the question or completes the statement. *PRINT THE LETTER OF THE CORRECT ANSWER IN THE SPACE AT THE RIGHT.*

1. A good magnetic material is

    A. aluminum   B. iron   C. brass   D. carbon

    1._____

2. A thermo-couple is a device for

    A. changing frequency
    B. changing d.c. to a.c.
    C. measuring temperature
    D. heat insulation

    2._____

3. It is desired to operate a 6-volt lamp from a 120-volt a.c. source. This can be done with the least waste power by using a

    A. series resistor   B. rectifier
    C. step-down transformer   D. rheostat

    3._____

4. Rosin is a material generally used

    A. in batteries
    B. as a dielectric
    C. as a soldering flux
    D. for high voltage insulation

    4._____

5. A milliampere is

    A. 1000 amperes   B. 100 amperes
    C. .01 ampere   D. .001 ampere

    5._____

6. A compound motor usually has

    A. only a shunt field
    B. only a series field
    C. no brushes
    D. both a shunt and a series field

    6._____

7. To connect a d.c. voltmeter to measure a voltage higher than the scale maximum, use a

    A. series resistance   B. shunt
    C. current transformer   D. voltage transformer

    7._____

8. The voltage applied to the terminals of a storage battery to charge it CANNOT be

    A. rectified a.c.   B. straight d.c.
    C. pulsating d.c.   D. ordinary a.c.

    8._____

9. When two unequal condensers are connected in parallel, the

    9._____

29

A. total capacity is decreased
B. total capacity is increased
C. result will be a short-circuit
D. smaller one will break down

10. A megohm is

    A. 10 ohms
    B. 100 ohms
    C. 1000 ohms
    D. 1,000,000 ohms

11. Of the following, the *POOREST* conductor of electricity is

    A. brass
    B. lead
    C. an acid solution
    D. slate

12. A flashlight battery, a condenser and a flashlight bulb are connected in series with each other. If the bulb burns brightly and steadily, then the condenser is

    A. open-circuited
    B. short-circuited
    C. good
    D. fully charged

13. A kilowatt of power will be taken from a 500-volt d.c. supply by a load of

    A. 200 amperes
    B. 20 amperes
    C. 2 amperes
    D. 0.2 ampere

14. A commutator is used on a shunt generator in order to

    A. step-up voltage
    B. step-up current
    C. change a.c. to d.c.
    D. control generator speed

15. The number of cells connected in series in a 6-volt storage battery of the lead-acid type is

    A. 2
    B. 3
    C. 4
    D. 5

16. A 15-ampere circuit breaker as compared to a 15-ampere plug fuse

    A. can be re-closed
    B. is cheaper
    C. is safer
    D. is smaller

17. Lengths of rigid conduit are connected together to make up a long run by means of

    A. couplings
    B. bushings
    C. hickeys
    D. lock nuts

18. BX is commonly used to indicate

    A. rigid conduit without wires
    B. flexible conduit without wires
    C. insulated wires covered with flexible steel armor
    D. insulated wires covered with a non-metallic covering

19. Good practice is to cut BX with a

    A. hacksaw
    B. 3-wheel pipe cutter
    C. bolt cutter
    D. heavy pliers

20. Silver is used for relay contacts in order to

A. improve conductivity B. avoid burning
C. reduce costs D. avoid arcing

21. Rigid conduit is fastened on the inside of the junction box by means of 21.____

    A. a bushing B. a locknut
    C. a coupling D. set-screw clamps

22. Of the following, the material which can best withstand high temperatures is 22.____

    A. plastic B. enamel C. fiber D. mica

23. A lead-acid type of storage battery exposed to freezing weather is most likely to freeze 23.____
    when

    A. the battery is fully charged
    B. the battery is completely discharged
    C. the water level is low
    D. the cap vent holes are plugged

24. An important reason making it poor practice to put telephone wires in the same conduit 24.____
    with a.c. power lines is that

    A. power will be lost from the a.c. line
    B. the conduit will overheat
    C. the wires may be confused
    D. the telephone circuits will be noisy

25. In a loaded power circuit, it is most dangerous to 25.____

    A. close the circuit with a circuit breaker
    B. close the circuit with a knife switch
    C. open the circuit with a knife switch
    D. open the circuit with a circuit breaker

26. When fastening electrical equipment to a hollow tile wall it is good practice to use 26.____

    A. toggle bolts B. wood screws
    C. nails D. ordinary bolts and nuts

27. Of the following, the most important reason for keeping the oil in a transformer tank mois- 27.____
    ture-free is to prevent

    A. rusting B. voltage breakdown
    C. freezing of the oil D. overheating

28. A voltmeter is generally connected to a high potential a.c. bus through 28.____

    A. an auto-transformer B. a potential transformer
    C. a resistor D. a relay

29. The highest total voltage which can be measured by using two identical 0-300 volt range 29.____
    meters connected in series would be

    A. 150 volts B. 300 volts
    C. 450 volts D. 600 volts

30. Transistors are mainly employed in electrical circuits to take the place of 30.____

A. resistors B. condensers
C. inductances D. vacuum tubes

31. The minimum number of 10-ohm, 1-ampere resistors which would be required to give an equivalent resistance of 10 ohms capable of carrying a 2-ampere load is

    A. 2 B. 3 C. 4 D. 5

32. To increase the current measuring range of an ammeter, the equipment commonly employed is a

    A. series resistor
    B. shunt
    C. short-circuiting switch
    D. choke

33. If a 10-watt lamp and a 100-watt lamp, each rated at 120 volts, are connected in series to a 240-volt source, then the voltage across the 10-watt lamp will be

    A. zero
    B. about 24 volts
    C. exactly 120 volts
    D. much more than 120 volts

34. If the load on the secondary of a small 10 to 1 step-up transformer is 100 watts, then the power being taken by the primary from the power line

    A. is less than 100 watts
    B. is exactly 100 watts
    C. is more than 100 watts
    D. may be more or less than 100 watts depending on the nature of the load

35. A 1/2-ohm, a 2-ohm, a 5-ohm and a 25-ohm resistor are connected in series to a power source. The resistor which will consume the most power is the

    A. 1/2-ohm B. 2-ohm C. 5-ohm D. 25-ohm

36. With respect to 60-cycle current, it is correct to say that one cycle takes

    A. 1/60th of a second B. 1/30th of a second
    C. 1/60th of a minute D. 1/30th of a minute

37. A rheostat is used in the field circuit of a shunt generator to control the

    A. generator speed B. load
    C. generator voltage D. power factor

Questions 38-45.
Questions 38 through 45 are based on the Subway Power Supply Information given below. Read this information carefully before answering these questions.

SUBWAY POWER SUPPLY INFORMATION

The subway train signal system derives its power from a 3-phase, 4-wire, 60-cycle a.c. source which has a phase to phase voltage of 208 volts and a voltage of 120 volts between each phase wire and the grounded neutral. The signal system power is taken from one phase wire and the grounded neutral and applied to the primary of a 1 to 1 transformer. The secondary of this transformer powers the signal main. Train propulsion power is 600 volts supplied from mercury arc rectifiers and fed to the 3rd rail, from which it is picked up by car contact shoes, taken through the car motors as required and returned through the car wheels and then through one of the running rails back to the power source. This rail, known as the negative propulsion current rail, has heavy bonds around each rail joint. The other running rail, known as the signal rail, has insulated rail joints at various intervals to separate one track signal circuit from another and the rail joints between insulated joints are bonded with relatively light bonds.

38. The voltage on the signal main is most nearly

    A. 600 volts d.c. B. 208 volts a.c.
    C. 120 volts a.c. D. 120 volts d.c.

39. The voltage on the contact shoes of the car is

    A. 600 volts d.c. B. 600 volts a.c.
    C. 208 volts a.c. D. 120 volts d.c.

40. It is apparent that the number of conductors in a signal main is

    A. one   B. two   C. three   D. four

41. Since the 1 to 1 transformer does not change the voltage, its purpose is to insulate

    A. the signal main from the 600-volt supply
    B. the signal main from the 3-phase source
    C. adjacent track circuits
    D. the 3rd rail from the running rail

42. Light bonds are provided on the rail joints of

    A. the 3rd rail
    B. both running rails
    C. one running rail
    D. the negative propulsion current rail

43. Track signal circuits are separated from other by

    A. rail bonds   B. ordinary rail joints
    C. a grounded neutral D. insulated rail joints

44. The negative return for the car motors is through

    A. the 3rd rail   B. the signal rail
    C. both running rails D. one running rail

45. If one insulated rail joint becomes short-circuited, then the number of track signal circuits affected will be

    A. one   B. two   C. three   D. four

46. If a condenser has a safe working voltage of 250 volts d.c., then it would be most likely to break down if used across

   A. a 250-volt, 60-cycle a.c. line
   B. a 250-volt d.c. line
   C. a 240-volt battery
   D. a 120-volt, 25-cycle a.c. line

46.____

47. Transformer cores are generally made up of thin steel laminations. The main purpose of this is to

   A. reduce the transformer losses
   B. reduce the initial cost of the transformer
   C. increase the weight of the transformer
   D. prevent voltage breakdown in the transformer

47.____

48. The main reason for using copper tips in soldering irons is because copper

   A. is a good heat conductor
   B. is a good electrical conductor
   C. has a low melting point
   D. is very soft

48.____

49. Five identical electric fans, each rated at 120 volts d.c. are connected in series with each other on a 600-volt circuit. If one fan develops an open circuit then

   A. the remaining fans will run, but at slow speed
   B. the remaining fans will run, but at above normal speed
   C. only one fan will run
   D. none of the fans will run

49.____

50. The pressure of a carbon brush on a commutator is measured with a

   A. spring balance B. feeler gage
   C. taper gage   D. wire gage

50.____

KEY (CORRECT ANSWERS)

1. B	11. D	21. A	31. C	41. B
2. C	12. B	22. D	32. B	42. C
3. C	13. C	23. B	33. D	43. D
4. C	14. C	24. D	34. C	44. D
5. D	15. B	25. C	35. D	45. B
6. D	16. A	26. A	36. A	46. A
7. A	17. A	27. B	37. C	47. A
8. D	18. C	28. B	38. C	48. A
9. B	19. A	29. D	39. A	49. D
10. D	20. A	30. D	40. B	50. A

TEST 2

DIRECTIONS: Each question or incomplete statement is followed by several suggested answers or completions. Select the one that BEST answers the question or completes the statement. *PRINT THE LETTER OF THE CORRECT ANSWER IN THE SPACE AT THE RIGHT.*

1. A non-inductive carbon resistor consumes 50 watts when connected across a 120-volt d.c. source. If it is connected across a 120-volt a.c. source, the power consumed by the resistor will be nearest to

   A. 30 watts B. 40 watts C. 50 watts D. 60 watts

   1.____

2. Of the following, the combination of lamps which will draw the most current from a standard 120-volt branch circuit is one with

   A. three 150-watt lamps
   B. one 300-watt lamp
   C. four 100-watt lamps
   D. six 50-watt lamps

   2.____

3. A condenser is sometimes connected across contact points which make and break a d.c. circuit in order to reduce arcing of the points. The condenser produces this effect because it

   A. discharges when the contacts open
   B. charges when the contacts open
   C. charges while the contacts are closed
   D. discharges when the contacts are closed

   3.____

4. One of the difficulties experienced with d.c. motors is "high mica." To correct this trouble, good practice is to

   A. use very soft commutator bars
   B. use very soft brushes
   C. undercut the mica
   D. use very narrow commutator bars

   4.____

5. A 120-volt a.c. generator has a full load rating of 12 kva. This means that full load current for this machine is

   A. 10 amperes
   B. 100 amperes
   C. 1000 amperes
   D. 10,000 amperes

   5.____

6. A power-factor meter would be used in

   A. a battery circuit
   B. a d.c. generator circuit
   C. an a.c. generator circuit
   D. a d.c. motor circuit

   6.____

7. Measurements of the air-gap clearance between the pole pieces and the armature of a motor are useful in determining wear of the

   A. commutator
   B. brushes
   C. bearings
   D. pole pieces

   7.____

35

8. Transit workers are cautioned not to leave tools on scaffolding. The most important reason for this rule is to

   A. prevent theft of the tools
   B. prevent mix-ups in the worker's tools
   C. prevent damage to tools
   D. avoid a safety hazard

9. Transit workers are advised to report injuries caused by nails, no matter how slight. The most important reason for this rule is that this type of injury

   A. is caused by violating safety rules
   B. can only be caused by carelessness
   C. generally causes dangerous bleeding
   D. may result in a serious infection

10. In connection with the use of a wire snale, it is NOT necessary to

    A. tape it when coiled
    B. avoid kinking
    C. grease it
    D. avoid contact with live circuits

11. The material discharged by a carbon dioxide fire extinguisher should not be handled because it

    A. can cause a frost-bite
    B. is a poisonous liquid
    C. is highly volatile
    D. is valuable for re-use

12. Aluminum is often used for transmission lines instead of copper because it

    A. is stronger
    B. is lighter
    C. has higher conductivity
    D. is non-corrosive

13. The colored lenses on the subway signals located along the trackway are replaced as quickly as possible if they are broken. The most important reason for doing this is probably to prevent

    A. misunderstanding of the signal by a motorman
    B. injuries from broken glass
    C. the signal lamp from burning out too quickly
    D. dirt from getting on the signal lamp

14. An important precaution in connection with electric welding is to

    A. avoid shock
    B. prevent overloading the machine
    C. protect the face and eyes
    D. wear loose clothes

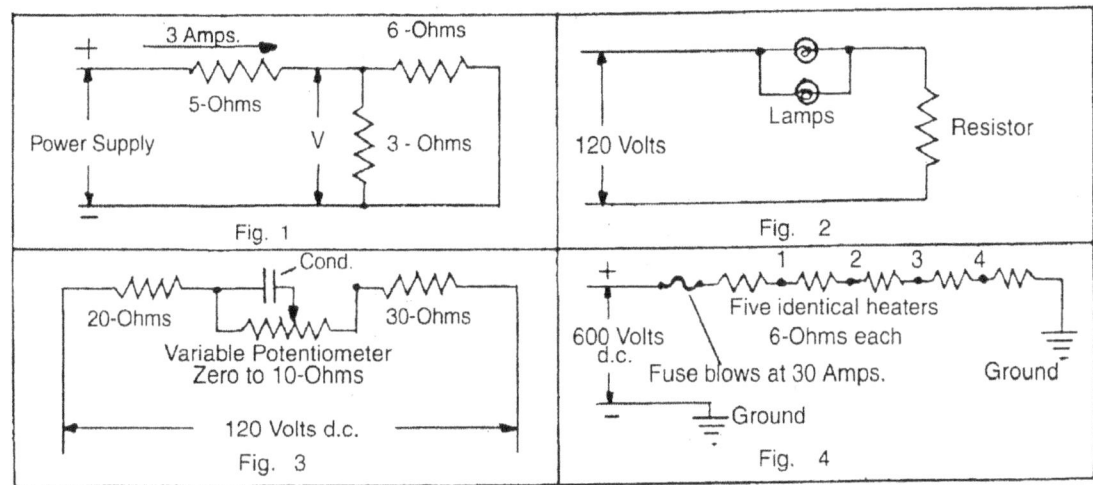

Questions 15 - 22.

Questions 15 through 22 refer to the figures above. Each question gives the proper figure to use with that question.

15. In Fig. 1, the voltage V is 15.____

    A. 27 volts   B. 9 volts   C. 6 volts   D. 3 volts

16. In Fig. 1, the current in the 6-ohm resistor is 16.____

    A. 3 amperes   B. 2 amperes
    C. 1.5 amperes   D. 1 ampere

17. In Fig. 2, each lamp is to take 1-ampere at 20 volts. The resistor should be 17.____

    A. 100 ohms   B. 80 ohms   C. 50 ohms   D. 40 ohms

18. In Fig. 3, the *MAXIMUM* voltage which can be placed across the condenser by varying the potentiometer is 18.____

    A. 120 volts   B. 60 volts
    C. 40 volts   D. 20 volts

19. In Fig. 3, the *MINIMUM* voltage which can be placed across the condenser by varying the potentiometer is 19.____

    A. 60 volts   B. 40 volts   C. 20 volts   D. zero volts

20. In Fig. 4, the heater circuit is normally completed through the two ground connections shown. If an accidental ground occurs at point 4, then the number of heaters which will heat up is 20.____

    A. five   B. four   C. one   D. none

21. In Fig. 4, the fuse will *NOT* blow with a ground at 21.____

    A. point 1   B. point 2   C. point 3   D. point 4

22. In Fig. 4, if a short occurs from point 2 to point 3, then the number of heaters which will heat up Is 22.____

    A. five   B. four   C. two   D. none

23. Of the following, the A.W.G. size of single conductor bare copper wire which has the lowest resistance per foot is   23.____

    A. #40   B. #10   C. #00   D. #0

24. The voltage output of 6 ordinary flashlight dry cells of the zinc-carbon type, when connected in parallel with each other, will be approximately   24.____

    A. 1.5 volts   B. 3 volts
    C. 9 volts   D. 12 volts

25. Full load current for a 5-ohm, 20-watt resistor is   25.____

    A. 4 amperes   B. 3 amperes
    C. 2 amperes   D. 1 ampere

26. An auto-transformer could NOT be used to   26.____

    A. step-up voltage   B. step-down voltage
    C. act as a choke coil   D. change a.c. frequency

27. Telephones are located alongside of the subway tracks for emergency use. The locations of these telephones are indicated by blue lights. The reason for selecting this color rather than green is that   27.____

    A. a blue light can be seen for greater distances
    B. blue lights are easier to buy
    C. green cannot be seen by a person who is colorblind
    D. green lights are used for train signals

28. Subway signal equipment such as junction boxes located in the subway are kept padlocked. The most important reason, for doing this is probably to   28.____

    A. prevent rubbish from accumulating in this equipment
    B. minimize the effects of train vibration on the equipment
    C. prevent tampering by unauthorized personnel
    D. protect the equipment from dampness

29. On your first day on the job as a helper, you are assigned to work with a maintainer. During the course of the work, you realize that the maintainer is about to violate a basic safety rule. In this case the best thing for you to do is to   29.____

    A. immediately call it to his attention
    B. say nothing until he actually violates this rule and then call it to his attention
    C. say nothing, but later report this action to the foreman
    D. walk away from him so that you will not become involved

30. Transit rules state that electrical maintainers must not permit other employees to replace lamps of authorized wattage with lamps of higher wattage in the working areas of such employees. The most likely reason for this rule is   30.____

    A. to keep the cost of electricity down
    B. to prevent such employees from injuring their eyes
    C. to avoid overloading lighting circuits
    D. that higher wattage lamps cost more

31. If you find that the fuse clip on one side of a fuse is much hotter than the fuse clip on the other side of this fuse, it would indicate

    A. that the fuse is rated too low
    B. that the fuse is rated too high
    C. that the load current is too high
    D. poor contact at the hot fuse clip

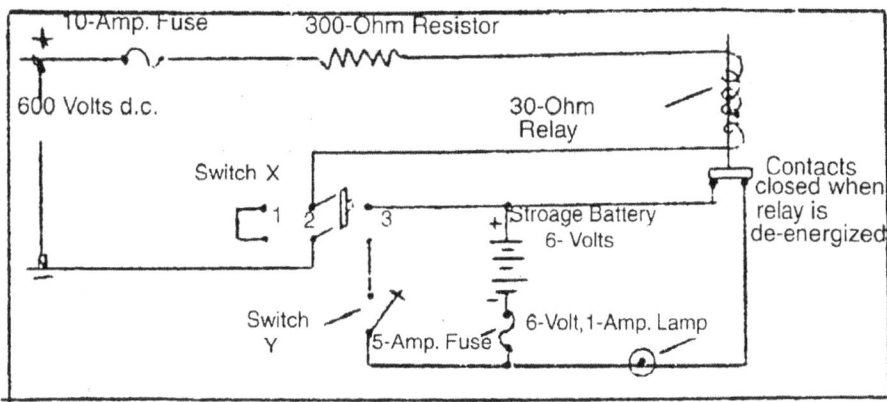

Questions 32 - 39.
Questions 32 through 39 are based on the above wiring diagram. Refer to this diagram when answering these questions.

32. Throwing switch X to Position No. 1 will

    A. charge the battery   B. energize the lamp
    C. energize the relay   D. blow the 5-ampere fuse

33. With switch X in Position No. 1, the 10-ampere fuse will blow if a dead short occurs across the

    A. 300-ohm resistor   B. relay coil
    C. battery   D. lamp

34. With switch X in Position No. 2, the current through the 300-ohm resistor will be

    A. zero   B. 2 amperes
    C. 2.2 amperes   D. 10 amperes

35. With switch X in Position No. 3, and switch Y open, the current taken from the battery will be

    A. zero   B. 1 ampere
    C. 5 amperes   D. 10 amperes

36. With switch Y in the open position and the relay contacts open,

    A. the lamp will be lit
    B. the lamp will be dark
    C. the battery will be discharging
    D. the 5-ampere fuse will be overloaded

37. The battery will charge with

A. switch X in Position No. 3 and switch Y closed
B. switch X in Position No. 3 and switch Y open
C. switch X in Position No. 1 and switch Y closed
D. switch X in Position No. 1 and switch Y open

38. With the relay contacts closed, a dead short across the lamp will

    A. blow the 10-ampere fuse
    B. blow the 5-ampere fuse
    C. not blow any fuses
    D. cause the battery to charge

39. When the switches are set to the positions which will charge the battery, the charging current will be approximately

    A. 1/2 ampere   B. 2 amperes
    C. 5 amperes   D. 10 amperes

40. The most important reason for NOT having a power line splice in a conduit run between boxes is that

    A. it will be impossible to pull the wires through
    B. this would be an unsafe practice
    C. the splice will heat up
    D. the splice would be hard to repair

41. Goggles would be LEAST necessary when

    A. recharging soda-acid fire extinguishers
    B. clipping stones
    C. putting electrolyte into an Edison battery
    D. scraping rubber insulation from a wire

42. A commutator and brushes will be found on

    A. an alternator
    B. a rotary converter
    C. a squirrel-cage induction motor
    D. a wound-rotor induction motor

43. In a house bell circuit, the push button for ringing the bell is generally connected in the secondary of the transformer feeding the bell. One reason for doing this is to

    A. save power
    B. keep line voltage out of the push button circuit
    C. prevent the bell from burning out
    D. prevent arcing of the vibrator contact points in the bell

44. If a 120-volt transformer is connected to a 120-volt d.c. source, then the

    A. secondary voltage will cause the transformer to break down
    B. secondary current will be excessive
    C. primary current will cause the transformer to overheat
    D. primary voltage will be too low for the transformer to operate properly

45. The Wheatstone Bridge which is used for measuring resistances has

    A. a galvanometer
    B. a wattmeter
    C. a foot-candle meter
    D. a frequency meter

46. A wire has a resistance of 1 ohm per 1000 feet. A piece of this wire 200 feet long will have a resistance of

    A. .002 ohm   B. .02 ohm   C. .2 ohm   D. .5 ohm

47. The lead sheath of a cable is for the purpose of protecting the cable from

    A. water damage
    B. temperature changes
    C. eddy currents
    D. kinking

48. There are only a few emergency lights provided for subway car illumination, when the main lights go out because of loss of 3rd rail power. The best reason for providing only a few emergency lights is that these lamps

    A. are fed from a battery supply
    B. burn for longer periods than the main lights
    C. are more difficult to replace than the main lights
    D. provide as much light as the main lights

49. Before conducting an insulation resistance test on large machines with a megger, it is considered good practice to ground the windings for about 15 minutes immediately prior to the test. The most likely reason for this is to

    A. allow the machine to cool down
    B. remove static electricity which may have accumulated during the running of the machine
    C. reduce hazard from lightning
    D. permit moisture to evaporate from the windings

50. Sediment in the cells of a storage battery will most likely tend to

    A. increase the voltage output
    B. increase the current output
    C. short the cells
    D. cause the battery to leak

KEY (CORRECT ANSWERS)

1. C	11. A	21. D	31. D	41. D
2. A	12. B	22. B	32. C	42. B
3. B	13. A	23. C	33. A	43. B
4. C	14. C	24. A	34. A	44. C
5. B	15. C	25. C	35. B	45. A
6. C	16. D	26. D	36. B	46. C
7. C	17. C	27. D	37. A	47. A
8. D	18. D	28. C	38. B	48. A
9. D	19. D	29. A	39. B	49. B
10. C	20. B	30. C	40. B	50. C

EXAMINATION SECTION
TEST 1

DIRECTIONS: Each question or incomplete statement is followed by several suggested answers or completions. Select the one that *BEST* answers the question or completes the statement. *PRINT THE LETTER OF THE CORRECT ANSWER IN THE SPACE AT THE RIGHT.*

1. A circular mil is a measure of

    A. area B. length C. volume D. weight

    1._____

2. In electrical tests, a megger is calibrated to read

    A. amperes B. ohms C. volts D. watts

    2._____

3. Metal cabinets for lighting circuits are grounded in order to

    A. save insulating material
    B. provide a return for the neutral current
    C. eliminate short circuits
    D. minimize the possibility of shock

    3._____

4. In an a.c. circuit containing only resistance, the power factor will be

    A. zero
    C. 50% leading
    B. 50% lagging
    D. 100%

    4._____

5. The size of fuse for a two-wire lighting circuit using No. 14 wire should not exceed

    A. 15 amperes
    C. 25 amperes
    B. 20 amperes
    D. 30 amperes

    5._____

6. When working near acid storage batteries, extreme care should be taken to guard against sparks mainly because a spark may

    A. cause an explosion
    B. set fire to the electrolyte
    C. short circuit a cell
    D. ignite the battery case

    6._____

7. If a blown fuse in an existing lighting circuit is replaced by another of the same rating which also blows, the proper maintenance procedure is to

    A. use a higher rating fuse
    B. cut out some of the outlets in the circuit
    C. check the circuit for grounds or shorts
    D. install a renewable fuse

    7._____

8. The number of fuses required in a three-phase four-wire branch circuit with grounded neutral is

    A. one B. two C. three D. four

    8._____

9. The electrodes of the common dry cell are carbon and

    A. zinc B. lead C. steel D. tin

    9._____

43

10. An electrician's hickey is used to

   A. strip insulation off wire
   B. pull cable through conduits
   C. thread metallic conduit
   D. bend metallic conduit

11. A group of wire sizes that is correctly arranged in order of *INCREASING* current-carrying capacity is

   A. 6; 12; 3/0
   B. 12; 6; 3/0
   C. 3/0; 12; 6
   D. 3/0; 6; 12

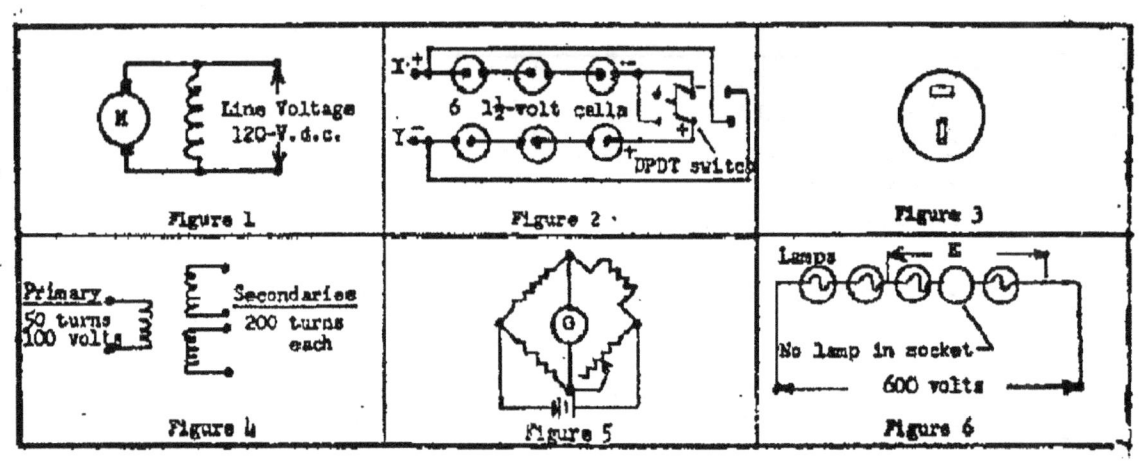

Questions 12 - 19.
Questions 12 through 19 refer to the figures above. Each question gives the proper figure to use with that question.

12. Figure 1 shows the standard diagram for

   A. a synchronous motor
   B. a shunt motor
   C. a series motor
   D. an induction motor

13. In Figure 1, if the line current is 5 amperes, the energy consumed by the motor if in continuous operation for 3 hours is

   A. 200 watthours
   B. 600 watthours
   C. 1800 watthours
   D. 9000 watthours

14. In Figure 2, with the DPDT switch closed to the right, the voltage between X and Y is

   A. 0
   B. 1 1/2
   C. 4 1/2
   D. 9

15. In Figure 2, with the DPDT closed to the left, the voltage between X and Y is

   A. 9
   B. 4 1/2
   C. 1 1/2
   D. 0

16. The convenience outlet shown in Figure 3 is used particularly for a device which

   A. is polarized
   B. is often disconnected
   C. takes a heavy current
   D. vibrates

17. In Figure 4, the *MAXIMUM* secondary voltage possible by interconnecting the secondaries is   17.____

    A. 50 volts   B. 200 volts
    C. 400 volts   D. 800 volts

18. Figure 5 shows a Wheatstone bridge which is used to measure   18.____

    A. voltage   B. resistance
    C. current   D. power

19. In Figure 6, with one of the five good lamps removed from its socket as indicated, the voltage is nearest to   19.____

    A. 240   B. 0   C. 600   D. 360

20. The metal which is the best conductor of electricity is   20.____

    A. silver   B. copper
    C. aluminum   D. nickel

21. If the two supply wires to a d.c. series motor are reversed, the motor will   21.____

    A. run in the opposite direction
    B. not run
    C. run in the same direction
    D. become a generator

22. Before doing work on a motor, to prevent accidental starting you should   22.____

    A. short circuit the motor leads
    B. remove the fuses
    C. block the rotor
    D. ground the frame

23. The material commonly used for brushes on d.c. motors is   23.____

    A. copper   B. carbon
    C. brass   D. aluminum

24. The conductors of a two-wire No. 12 armored cable used in an ordinary lighting circuit are   24.____

    A. stranded and rubber insulated
    B. solid and rubber insulated
    C. stranded and cotton insulated
    D. solid and cotton insulated

25. The rating, 125 V.-10A., 250 V.-5A., commonly applies to a   25.____

    A. snap switch   B. lamp
    C. conductor   D. fuse

26. Commutators are found on   26.____

    A. alternators   B. d.c. motors
    C. transformers   D. circuit breakers

27. A proper use for an electrician's knife is to

    A. cut wires
    B. pry out a small cartridge fuse
    C. mark the placd where a conduit is to be cut
    D. skin wires

28. A d.c. device taking one milliampere at one kilovolt takes a total power of

    A. one milliwatt
    B. one watt
    C. one kilowatt
    D. one megawatt

29. In connection with electrical work, it is good practice to

    A. scrape the silvery coating from a wire before soldering
    B. nick a wire in several places before bending it around a terminal
    C. assume that a circuit is alive
    D. open a switch to check the load

30. Mica is commonly used as an insulation

    A. for cartridge fuse cases
    B. between commutator bars
    C. between lead acid battery plates
    D. between transformer steel laminations

31. The function of a step-down transformer is to decrease the

    A. voltage
    B. current
    C. power
    D. frequency

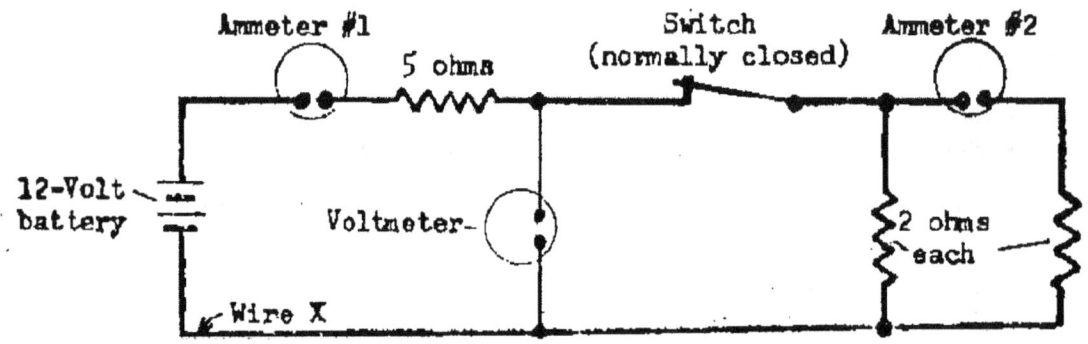

Questions 32-39.
Questions 32 through 39 refer to the circuit above. Neglect the effects of the various meters on the circuit.

32. The three resistors connected as shown have an equivalent resistance of

    A. 9 ohms   B. 7 ohms   C. 6 ohms   D. 4 ohms

33. When ammeter #1 indicates 2 amperes, ammeter #2 will indicate

    A. 1 ampere
    B. 2 amperes
    C. 3 amperes
    D. 4 amperes

5 (#1)

34. If the two wires to ammeter #1 are reversed the 34.____

    A. ammeter needle will move backwards
    B. ammeter needle will indicate zero
    C. ammeter will burn out
    D. current in the rest of the circuit will be reversed

35. With the switch either open or closed, the current in wire X is 35.____

    A. greater than in ammeter #1
    B. less than in ammeter #1
    C. the same as in ammeter #2
    D. the same as in ammeter #1

36. When ammeter #1 indicates 2 amperes, the power consumed by the 5-ohm resistor is 36.____

    A. 2.5 watts   B. 10 watts
    C. 20 watts   D. 50 watts

37. The highest voltage measured anywhere in the circuit is across the 37.____

    A. 5-ohm resistor   B. No. 1 ammeter
    C. battery   D. closed switch

38. If the normally-closed switch is opened, the meter that would still show an appreciable reading is 38.____

    A. the voltmeter   B. ammeter #1
    C. ammeter #2   D. none

39. The device in the circuit which undoubtedly has the highest resistance is the 39.____

    A. battery   B. 5-ohm resistor
    C. No. 1 ammeter   D. voltmeter

40. A conduit run is most often terminated in 40.____

    A. a coupling   B. an elbow
    C. a bushing   D. an outlet box

41. In long conduit runs, pull boxes are sometimes installed at intermediate points to 41.____

    A. avoid using couplings
    B. support the conduit
    C. make use of short lengths of conduit
    D. facilitate pulling wire

42. A rheostat would LEAST likely be used in connection with the operation of 42.____

    A. transformers   B. motors
    C. generators   D. battery charging M.G. sets

43. The fiber bushing inserted at the end of a piece of flexible metallic conduit prevents 43.____

    A. moisture from entering the cable
    B. the rough edges from cutting the insulation
    C. the wires from touching each other
    D. the wires from slipping back into the armor

44. Portable lamp cord is most likely to have

   A. paper insulation
   B. solid wire
   C. armored wire
   D. stranded wire

45. Thermal relays are used in motor circuits to protect against

   A. reverse current
   B. overspeed
   C. overvoltage
   D. overload

46. It is good practice to connect the ground wire for a building electrical system to a

   A. vent pipe
   B. steam pipe
   C. cold water pipe
   D. gas pipe

47. A good magnetic material is

   A. brass   B. copper   C. silver   D. iron

48. The most practical way to determine in the field the approximate length of insulated wire in a large coil is to

   A. unreel the wire and measure it with a 6-foot rule
   B. find another coil with the length marked on it and compare
   C. count the turns and multiply by the average circumference
   D. weigh the coil and compare it with a 1000-ft. coil

49. When the connections for a d.c. voltmeter are moved from one test point to another, the needle moves backwards. This means that the

   A. second test point is a.c.
   B. meter is defective
   C. meter is magnetized
   D. meter leads are reversed

50. A good insulating material that can be machined readily to a required shape is

   A. mica
   B. porcelain
   C. bakelite
   D. varnished cambric

KEY (CORRECT ANSWERS)

1. A	11. B	21. C	31. A	41. D
2. B	12. B	22. B	32. C	42. A
3. D	13. C	23. B	33. A	43. B
4. D	14. C	24. B	34. A	44. D
5. A	15. A	25. A	35. D	45. D
6. A	16. A	26. B	36. C	46. C
7. C	17. D	27. D	37. C	47. D
8. C	18. B	28. B	38. A	48. C
9. A	19. C	29. C	39. D	49. D
10. D	20. A	30. B	40. D	50. C

TEST 2

DIRECTIONS: Each question or incomplete statement is followed by several suggested answers or completions. Select the one that *BEST* answers the question or completes the statement. *PRINT THE LETTER OF THE CORRECT ANSWER IN THE SPACE AT THE RIGHT.*

1. In most cases, the logical and proper source from which you should first seek explanation of one of the transit rules you do not understand would be the

    A. Transit Authority
    B. head of your department
    C. maintainer with whom you are assigned to work
    D. helper who has an assignment similar to your own

2. Employees of the transit system whose work requires them to enter upon the tracks in the subway are cautioned not to wear loose fitting clothing. The *MOST* important reason for this caution is that loose fitting clothing may

    A. interfere when men are using heavy tools
    B. catch on some projection of a passing train
    C. tear more easily than snug fitting clothing
    D. give insufficient protection against subway dust

3. Your work will probably be *MOST* appreciated by your superior if you show that

    A. you like your work by asking all the questions you can about it
    B. you're on the job by keeping him informed whenever you think someone has violated a rule
    C. you're interested in improving the job by continually coming to him with suggestions
    D. you're willing to do your share by completing assigned tasks properly and on time

4. On the rapid transit system, it would be *MOST* logical to expect to find floodlights located in

    A. subway storage rooms
    B. maintenance headquarters
    C. outdoor train storage yards
    D. under-river tunnels

5. The most important reason for insisting on neatness in maintenance quarters is that it

    A. keeps the men busy in slack periods
    B. prevents tools from becoming rusty
    C. makes a good impression on visitors and officials
    D. decreases the chances of accidents to employees

6. Maintenance workers whose duties require them to work on the tracks in the subway generally work in pairs. The *LEAST* likely of the following possible reasons for this practice is that

    A. some of the work requires two men
    B. the men can help each other in case of accident

C. there is too much equipment for one man to carry
D. it protects against vandalism

7. A foreman reprimands a helper for walking across the subway tracks unnecessarily in violation of the rules and regulations. The BEST reaction of the helper in this situation is to

   A. tell the foreman that he was careful and that he did not take any chances
   B. explain that he took this action to save time
   C. keep quiet and accept the criticism
   D. demand that the foreman show him the rule he violated

7.____

8. The type of screwdriver which will develop the greatest turning force is a

   A. screwdriver-bit and brace
   B. spiral push-type
   C. standard straight handle
   D. straight handle with ratchet

8.____

9. The book of rules and regulations states that employees must give notice in person or by telephone of their intention to be absent from work at least one hour before they are scheduled to report for duty. The MOST logical reason for having this rule is so that

   A. the employee's excuse can be checked
   B. the employee's pay can be stopped for that day
   C. a substitute can be provided
   D. absences will be limited to necessary ones

9.____

10. In a shop, it would be most necessary to provide a fitted cover on the metal container for

    A. old paint brushes   B. oily ragsa nd waste
    C. sand   D. broken glass

10.____

11. A vertical cylindrical tank 4 feet in diameter and 5 feet high has a capacity of 470 gallons. The number of gallons in the tank when filled to a depth of 1'6" is nearest to

    A. 45   B. 95   C. 140   D. 180

11.____

12. A crate contains 3 pieces of equipment weighing 43, 59, and 66 pounds respectively. If the crate is lifted by 4 men each lifting one corner of the crate, the average number of pounds lifted by each of the men is

    A. 56   B. 51   C. 42   D. 36

12.____

13. The principal objection to using water from a hose to put out a fire involving electrical equipment is that

    A. serious shock may result
    B. metal parts may rust
    C. fuses may blow out
    D. it may spread the fire

13.____

14. Maintainers of the transit system are required to report defective equipment to their superiors, even when the maintenance of the particular equipment is handled by another bureau. The purpose of this rule is to

14.____

A. punish employees who don't do their jobs
B. have repairs made before serious trouble occurs
C. keep employees on their toes
D. reward those who keep their eyes open

15. When summoning an ambulance for an injured person, it is most important to give the

    A. name of the injured person
    B. nature of the injuries
    C. cause of the accident
    D. location of the injured person

16. Employees using supplies from one of the first aid kits available throughout the subway are required to submit an immediate report of the occurrence. Logical reasoning shows that the most important purpose for this report is so that the

    A. supplies used will be sure to be replaced
    B. first aid kit can be properly sealed again
    C. employee will be credited for his action
    D. record of first aid supplies will be up to date

17. The tool shown at the right is used to

    A. set nails
    B. set lead anchors
    C. drill holes in concrete
    D. centerpunch for holes

18. The tool shown at the right is a
    A. punch
    B. Phillips-type screwdriver
    C. drill holder
    D. socket wrench

19. The tool shown at the right is
    A. an Allen-head wrench
    B. an offset screwdriver
    C. a double scraper
    D. a nail puller

20. The tool shown at the right is
    A. an offset wrench
    B. a spanner wrench
    C. a box wrench
    D. an open end wrench

21. The tool shown at the right is used to
    A. ream holes in wood
    B. countersink holes in soft metals
    C. turn Phillips-head screws
    D. drill holes in concrete

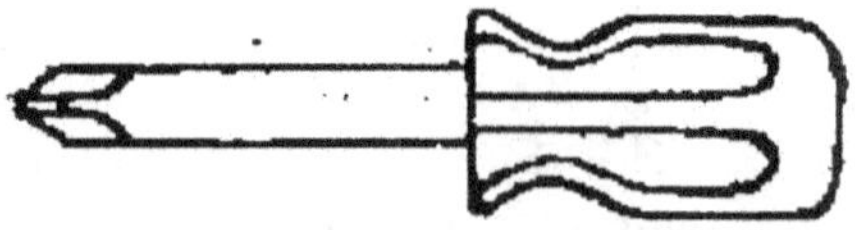

22. If the head of a hammer has become loose on the handle, it should properly be tightened by

   A. driving the handle further into the head
   B. using a slightly larger wedge
   C. driving a nail alongside the present wedge
   D. soaking the handle in water

23. The right angle shown has been divided into three parts. The number of degrees in the unmarked part is
   A. 46
   B. 36
   C. 21
   D. 6

24. Assume that you have burned your hand accidentally while on the job. The POOREST first aid remedy for the burn would be

   A. tannic acid
   B. iodine
   C. vaseline
   D. baking soda

25. The decimal which is nearest 33/64 is

   A. 0.516
   B. 0.500
   C. 34/64
   D. 1.939

26. A rule of the transit system is that the telephone must not be used for personal calls. The most important reason for this rule is that the added personal calls

   A. require additional operators
   B. waste company time
   C. tie up telephones which may be urgently needed for company business
   D. increase telephone maintenance

27. The main purpose of period inspections made by the maintainers on transit system equipment is probably to

   A. encourage the men to take better care of the equipment
   B. discover minor faults before they develop into serious breakdowns
   C. make the men familiar with the equipment
   D. keep the maintenance men busy during otherwise slack periods

28. A maintainer puts in the following order, "standard stranded, No. 1 gage, bare, galvanized, high strength, steel wire." The required missing information is the

   A. length
   B. diameter
   C. type
   D. material

29. A coil-spring one foot long has a mark 3 inches from the left end. If this spring is stretched from one end to the other of a yardstick, the mark will be at

   A. 1" on yardstick
   B. 3" on yardstick
   C. 9" on yardstick
   D. 12" on yardstick

30. There is a series of holes along a straight line in a piece. The first hole is 1", the second hole is 3/4", the 3rd is 1/2" and the 4th is 1/4". "If this pattern repeats continuously, the 10th hole is

   A. 1"   B. 3/4"   C. 1/2"   D. 1/4"

31. A rule of the transit system states that, "In walking on the track, walk opposite to the direction of traffic on that track if possible." By logical reasoning, the principal safety idea behind this rule is that the man on the track

   A. is more likely to see an approaching train
   B. will be seen more readily by the motorman
   C. need not be as careful
   D. is better able to judge the speed of the train

32. From your observation and knowledge of the subway, the logical reason that certain employees who work on the tracks carry small parts in fiber pails rather than steel pails is that fiber pails

   A. are stronger
   B. can't rust
   C. can't be dented by rough usage
   D. do not conduct electricity

33. When you are newly assigned as a helper to an experienced maintainer, he is most likely to give you good training if your attitude is that

   A. you need the benefit of his experience
   B. he is responsible for your progress
   C. you have the basic knowledge but lack the details
   D. he should do the job where little is to be learned

34. An employee will most likely avoid accidental injury if he

   A. stops to rest frequently
   B. works alone
   C. keeps mentally alert
   D. works very slowly

35. When making a piping or conduit installation, small steel pipe is best turned by using a

   A. monkey wrench   B. stillson wrench
   C. spanner wrench   D. chain wrench

36. A box contains an equal number of iron and brass castings. Each iron casting weighs 2 pounds and each brass casting one pound. If the box contents weigh 240 lbs., the number of brass pieces in the box is

   A. 40   B. 80   C. 120   D. 160

37. The sum of 5 feet 2-3/4 inches, 8 feet 1/2 inch, and 12-1/2 inches is

   A. 25 feet 3-3/4 inches   B. 14 feet 3-3/4 inches
   C. 13 feet 5-3/4 inches   D. 13 feet 3-3/4 inches

38. It ordinarily requires 5 days for 2 men to complete a certain job. If the management wants to have this work done in two days, the number of men required would be

    A. 10   B. 7   C. 6   D. 5

38.____

39. If your maintainer makes contact with a 600-volt conductor and remains in contact, your first action should be to

    A. search for the disconnecting switch
    B. ground the conductor with a bare wire
    C. pull him loose by his clothing
    D. cut the conductor

39.____

40. Before using an electric drill to make a hole in a piece of scrap iron, it is best to mark the location of the hole with a center punch in order to

    A. make the location easier to see
    B. keep the drill from wandering
    C. C . eliminate the need for a marking device
    D. keep the fuse from blowing

40.____

41. Small cuts or injuries should be

    A. taken care of immediately to avoid infection
    B. ignored because they are seldom important
    C. ignored unless they are painful
    D. taken care of at the end of the day

41.____

42. If you feel that one of your co-workers is not doing his share of the work, your best procedure is to

    A. increase your own output as a good example
    B. reduce your work output to bring this matter to a head
    C. point this out to the foreman
    D. take no action and continue to do your job properly

42.____

43. In case of accident, employees who witnessed the accident are required by the rules to make *INDIVIDUAL* written reports on prescribed forms as soon as possible. The most logical reason for requiring such individual reports rather than a single joint report signed by all witnesses is because the individual reports are

    A. more likely to result in decreasing the number of accidents
    B. less likely to be lost at the same time
    C. less likely to contain unnecessary information
    D. more likely to give the complete picture

43.____

44. If a helper finds two orders on his headquarters bulletin board giving conflicting instructions with regard to his work, his most helpful action would be to

    A. call it to the attention of his superior
    B. comply with the order which is easier to follow
    C. follow the order which is best in his judgment
    D. defer that part of the work until a clarifying order is posted

44.____

45. The purpose of giving certain transit employees training in first aid is to

   A. provide temporary emergency aid
   B. eliminate the need for calling doctors in accident cases
   C. save money
   D. decrease the number of accidents

46. When you are first appointed as a helper and are assigned to work with a maintainer, he will probably expect you to

   A. make plenty of mistakes
   B. do very little work
   C. do all of the unpleasant work
   D. pay close attention to instructions

47. According to a safety report, a frequent cause of accidents to workers is the improper use of tools. The most helpful conclusion that you can draw from this statement is that

   A. most tools are difficult to use properly
   B. most tools are dangerous to use
   C. many accidents from tools are unavoidable
   D. many accidents from tools occur because of poor working habits

48. The best way to locate a point on the floor directly below the center of a hole in the ceiling is to use a

   A. plumb bob
   B. measuring tape
   C. folding rule
   D. center punch

49. It is generally known that the voltage of the third rail on the New York City subway system is about

   A. 120   B. 600   C. 1000   D. 3000

50. Roadside equipment associated with rapid transit railroad operation is generally housed in a cast iron case. The case is so designed that a gasket is compressed between the door edges and the door frame when the door is locked. By logical reasoning, it is clear that the principal purpose of the gasket is to

   A. act as a cushion to prevent cracking of the cast iron
   B. seal the case so dust and water cannot enter
   C. protect the equipment in the case against vibration
   D. prevent the door from becoming sealed tight by rust

KEY (CORRECT ANSWERS)

1. C	11. C	21. C	31. A	41. A
2. B	12. C	22. B	32. D	42. D
3. D	13. A	23. B	33. A	43. D
4. C	14. B	24. B	34. C	44. A
5. D	15. D	25. A	35. B	45. A
6. D	16. A	26. C	36. B	46. D
7. C	17. C	27. B	37. B	47. D
8. A	18. D	28. A	38. D	48. A
9. C	19. B	29. C	39. C	49. B
10. B	20. D	30. B	40. B	50. B

EXAMINATION SECTION
TEST 1

DIRECTIONS: Each question or incomplete statement is followed by several suggested answers or completions. Select the one that *BEST* answers the question or completes the statement. *PRINT THE LETTER OF THE CORRECT ANSWER IN THE SPACE AT THE RIGHT.*

1. The one of the following which could *NOT* be correctly used in describing a toggle switch is

    A. single-hole mounting
    B. slow-acting
    C. three-way
    D. double-pole

2. The flexible power cord connected to a portable tool is sure to have

    A. steel armor
    B. stranded wires
    C. aluminum
    D. asbestos insulation

3. The conductors in a large lead-covered telephone cable are usually

    A. stranded and rubber insulated
    B. solid and rubber insulated
    C. stranded and paper insulated
    D. solid and paper insulated

4. The rating-terms "240 volts, 10 H.P." would be properly used as part of the specifications for

    A. transformers
    B. motors
    C. storage batteries
    D. heaters

5. To measure the power taken by a d.c. electric motor with only a single instrument you should use

    A. a voltmeter
    B. an ammeter
    C. a wattmeter
    D. a power factor meter

6. Wire splices in modern home and business building wiring systems are made both mechanically firm and of low resistance by means of

    A. mechanical connectors
    B. spot welding
    C. brazing
    D. plastic tape

7. From your knowledge of electrical equipment you know that the part of a transformer which is most subject to damage from high temperature is the

    A. iron core
    B. copper winding
    C. winding insulation
    D. frame or case

8. The power factor of an a.c. circuit containing both a resistor and a condenser is

    A. 0
    B. between 0 and 1.0
    C. 1.0
    D. between 1.0 and 2.0

9. The material *NOT* likely to be found in use as insulation on electrical wires and cables is

    A. varnished cambric
    B. paper
    C. glazed porcelain
    D. asbestos

10. Lighting of many of the subway stations is provided by groups of 5 lamps. Each group of 5 lamps is connected in series and each lamp is rated at 130 volts.
    For full voltage burning of the lamps, the voltage of the supply which feeds these circuits must be

    A. 650 volts
    B. 260 volts
    C. 130 volts
    D. 26 volts

11. Recent safety reports indicate that a principal cause of injury to transit employees is "falls" while on the job. Such reports tend to emphasize that safety on the job is best assured by

    A. following every rule
    B. keeping alert
    C. never working alone
    D. working very slowly

12. The one of the following statements about a plug fuse that is most valid is that it should

    A. always be screwed in lightly to assure easy removal
    B. never be used to hold a coin in the fuse socket
    C. never be replaced by someone unfamiliar with the circuit
    D. always be replaced by a larger size if it burns out frequently

13. The circumference of a circle is given by the formula $C = \pi D$, where C is the circumference, D is the diameter and π is about 3 1/7. If a coil of 20 turns of wire has an average diameter of 16 inches, the total length of wire on the coil is nearest to

    A. 45 feet
    B. 65 feet
    C. 75 feet
    D. 85 feet

14. When the level of the liquid in a storage battery cell is too low, the proper liquid to add to bring the level up to normal is

    A. alkaline solution
    B. distilled water
    C. acid solution
    D. alcohol

15. Mercury toggle switches are sometimes used instead of regular toggle switches because they

    A. cost less
    B. are lighter
    C. are easier to install
    D. do not wear out as quickly

16. When a 100-watt, 120-volt lamp burns continuously for 8 hours at rated voltage the energy used is

    A. 800 watt-hours
    B. 960 watt-hours
    C. 12,000 watt-hours
    D. 96,000 watt-hours

17. Lead is the metal commonly used for

    A. transformer cores
    B. storage battery plates
    C. knife-switch blades
    D. power station panel boards

18. The term "60-watt" is most commonly used in identifying a

    A. fuse
    B. lamp
    C. cable
    D. switch

19. If the input to a 10 to 1 step-down transformer is 25 amperes at 12,000 volts, the secondary output would be nearest to

    A. 2.5 amperes at 12,000 volts
    B. 250 amperes at 120 volts
    C. 2.5 amperes at 120 volts
    D. 250 amperes at 12,000 volts

19.____

20. The plug fuse protecting a 120-volt circuit blows because of a dead short-circuit. If, while the short-circuit remains, a 120-volt lamp is screwed into the fuse socket in place of the burned out fuse, the lamp will

    A. burn dimly   B. remain dark
    C. burn out   D. burn normally

20.____

21. The number of 1 1/2-volt dry cells that must be connected in series to obtain 9 volts is

    A. 3   B. 4   C. 6   D. 9

21.____

22. Artificial respiration after a severe electric shock is always necessary when the shock results in

    A. unconsciousness   B. a burn
    C. stoppage of breathing D. bleeding

22.____

23. When wire splices are soldered, a flux is used before the solder is applied. The purpose of the flux is to

    A. make the solder adhere readily to the wire
    B. reduce the amount of heat required to melt the solder
    C. save solder
    D. make it unnecessary to clean the wires after skinning

23.____

24. A 600-volt cartridge fuse is most easily distinguished from a 250-volt cartridge fuse of the same current rating by its

    A. brass ferrules   B. smaller diameter
    C. greater length   D. oval shape

24.____

25. The best way for you, as a maintalner's helper, to cooperate with your maintainer is by

    A. doing the work assigned to you to the best of your ability
    B. continually suggesting new Ideas
    C. using your best judgment on a job even if in doubt as to a procedure
    D. constantly asking questions about the various phases of the work

25.____

26. An electrical helper notices that a certain relay does not pick up promptly when its control circuit is closed. Of the following faults, the only one that could be the cause of this delayed operation is a

    A. control wire broken off one of the relay terminals
    B. burned out fuse
    C. burned out relay coil
    D. fuse making poor contact

26.____

27. The principal objection to using water from a hose to put out a fire involving live electrical equipment is that

    A. insulation may be damaged
    B. cast iron parts may rust
    C. serious electric shock may result
    D. a short-circuit will result

27.____

28. If a standard incandescent electric lamp is operated at slightly more than its rated voltage the results will be

    A. shorter life and less light
    B. longer life but less light
    C. shorter life but more light
    D. longer life and more light

28.____

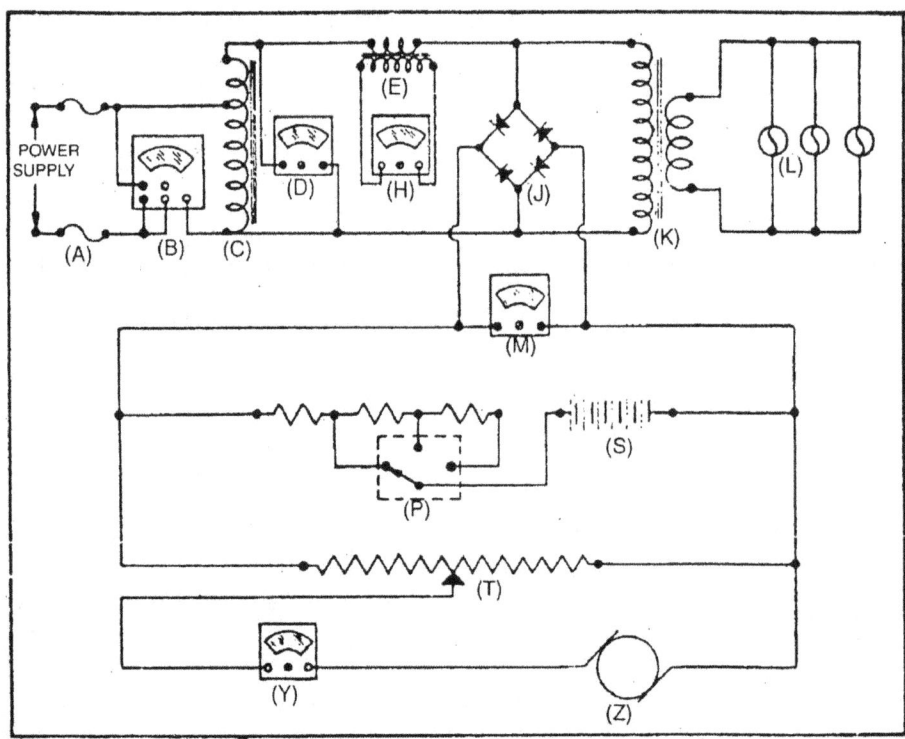

Questions 29 - 40.

Questions 29 through 40 are the names of various electrical devices and measuring instruments each of which is represented by one of the symbols in the above diagram. For each item below, select the appropriate symbol from the diagram. *PRINT*, in the correspondingly numbered item space at the right, the letter given below your selected symbol.

29. lamps   29.____

30. tap switch   30.____

31. battery   31.____

32. d.c. ammeter   32.____

33. d.c. voltmeter   33._____

34. potentiometer   34._____

35. auto-transformer   35._____

36. wattmeter   36._____

37. rectifier   37._____

38. a.c. voltmeter   38._____

39. fuse   39._____

40. a.c. ammeter   40._____

Questions 41 - 50.
Questions 4l through 50 refer to the use of tools shown in the diagram on the next page. Read the item, and for the operation given, select the proper tool to be used from those shown. *PRINT,* in the correspondingly numbered item space at the right, the letter given below your selected tool.

41. Tightening a coupling on the end of a piece of conduit   41._____

42. Making a hole in a concrete wall for a lead anchor   42._____

43. Cutting a one-inch conduit   43._____

44. Loosening the wire connection on the terminal of a standard electric light socket   44._____

45. Cutting 3/0 insulated copper cable   45._____

46. Measuring the total length of several coupled pieces of straight conduit behind a live switchboard without an assistant   46._____

47. Cutting a piece of #10 bare copper wire   47._____

48. Cleaning the burrs from the end of a piece of conduit after cutting   48._____

49. Tightening the drill in the chuck of an electric drill   49._____

50. Tightening the nut on a small stud terminal   50._____

6 (#1)

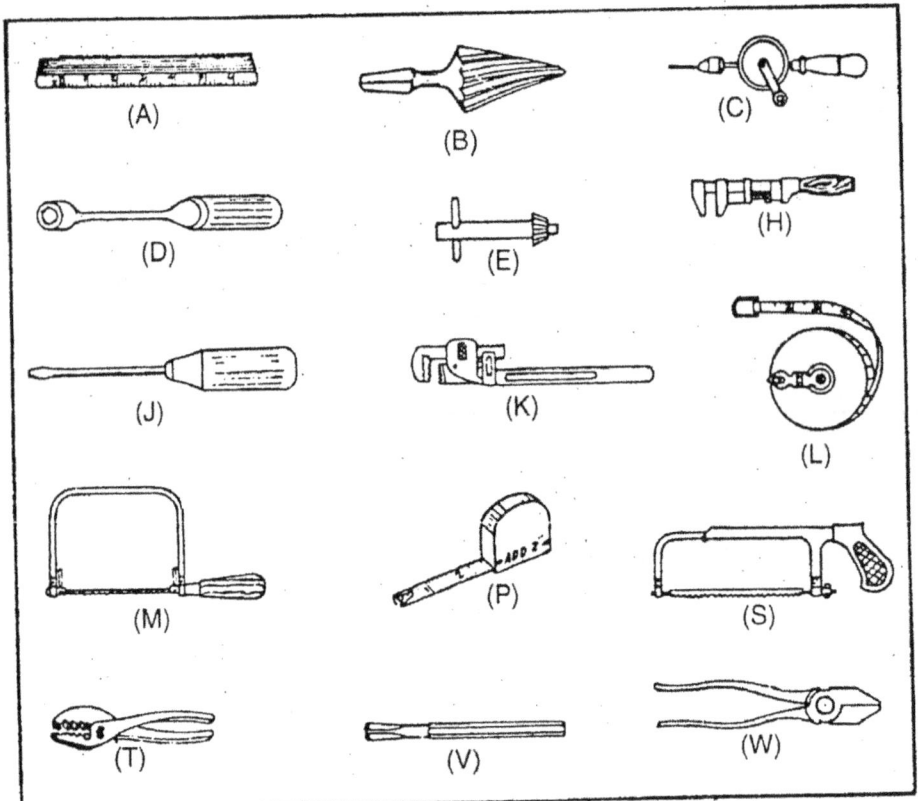

KEY (CORRECT ANSWERS)

1. B	11. B	21. C	31. S	41. K
2. B	12. B	22. C	32. Y	42. V
3. D	13. D	23. A	33. M	43. S
4. B	14. B	24. C	34. T	44. J
5. C	15. D	25. A	35. C	45. S
6. A	16. A	26. D	36. B	46. A
7. C	17. B	27. C	37. J	47. W
8. B	18. B	28. C	38. D	48. B
9. C	19. B	29. L	39. A	49. E
10. A	20. D	30. P	40. H	50. D

TEST 2

DIRECTIONS: Each question or incomplete statement is followed by several suggested answers or completions. Select the one that BEST answers the question or completes the statement. PRINT THE LETTER OF THE CORRECT ANSWER IN THE SPACE AT THE RIGHT.

1. When a long thread is used on one of two pieces of conduit joined by a coupling secured with a lock nut as indicated in the sketch, the probable reason for the use of this long thread is that
   A. one piece of conduit has been cut too short
   B. expansion or contraction of conduit due to temperature changes has to be compensated for
   C. neither conduit was free to turn when the coupling was made
   D. the joint has to be firmly anchored in a concrete wall

1.____

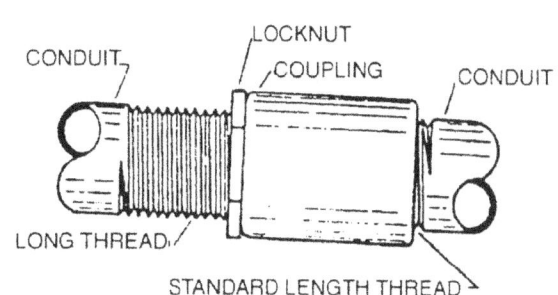

2. The flat-head screw is No.
   A. 1
   B. 2
   C. 3
   D. 4

2.____

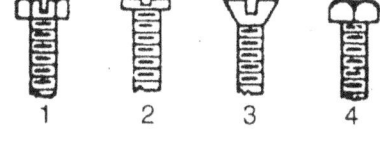

3. The "Phillips" head is No.
   A. 1
   B. 2
   C. 3
   D. 4

3.____

4. If the upper fuse is good and the lower fuse is burned out, the test lamp that will be lighted is No.
   A. 1
   B. 2
   C. 3
   D. 4

4.____

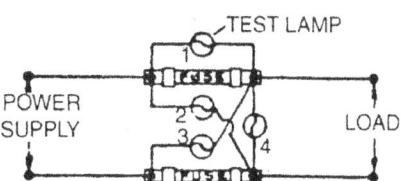

5. Assume you have decided to test a sealed box having two terminals by using the hookup shown. When you hold the test prods on the terminals, the voltmeter needle swings upscale and then quickly returns to zero. As an initial conclusion you would be correct in assuming that the box contained a

5.____

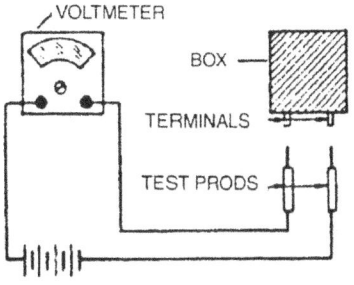

   A. condenser   B. choke   C. rectifier   D. resistor

6. Each of the four resistors shown has a resistance of 50 ohms. If the second resistor from the left becomes open-circuited, the reading of the voltmeter will
   A. increase slightly
   B. decrease slightly
   C. fall to zero
   D. become 240 volts

6._____

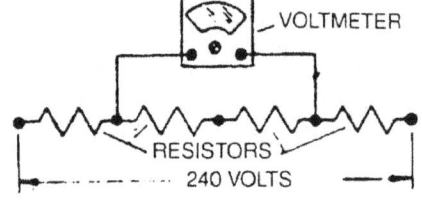

7. The reading of the ammeter should be
   A. 4.0
   B. 2.0
   C. 1.0
   D. 0.5

7._____

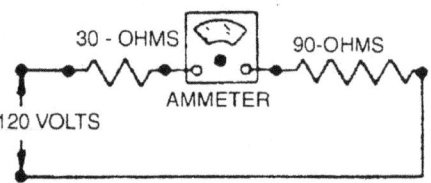

8. The reading of the voltmeter should be nearest to
   A. 30
   B. 90
   C. 120
   D. 240

8._____

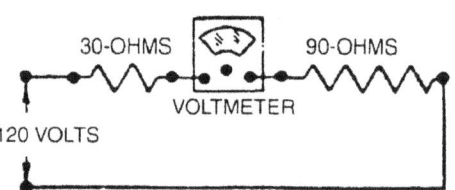

9. The resistor that carries the most current is the one whose resistance, in ohms, is
   A. 4
   B. 3
   C. 2
   D. 1

9._____

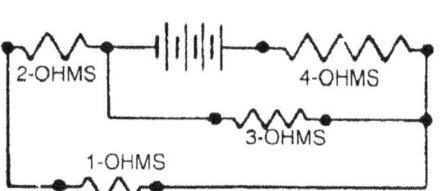

10. The reading of the voltmeter will be highest when the test prods are held on points
    A. 1 and 4
    B. 2 and 5
    C. 3 and 6
    D. 4 and 7

10._____

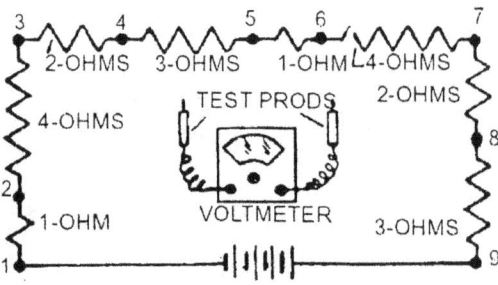

11. The two small a.c. motors are identical, but pinion #2 has twice the diameter of pinion #1. The motors are connected to the same power supply and are wired so that they normally tend to turn in *OPPOSITE* directions. When the power is first turned on

11._____

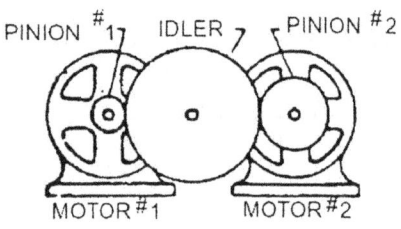

   A. the motors will stall
   B. both motors will turn at near normal speed in the same direction
   C. motor #2 will turn in its normal direction driving motor #1 backwards
   D. motor #1 will turn in its normal direction driving motor #2 backwards

12. Applying your knowledge of electrical measuring instruments, it is most likely that the scale shown is for

    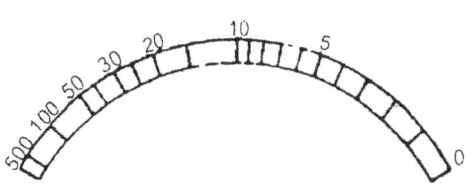

    A. an ohmmeter
    B. a voltmeter
    C. an ammeter
    D. a wattmeter

13. The diameter of the cable, compared to the diameter of a single conductor, is between

    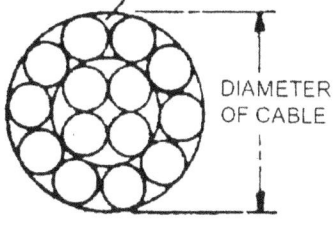

    A. two and three times
    B. three and four times
    C. four and five times
    D. five and six times

14. Compared to the total resistance of the variable resistor, the resistance between terminals 1 and 2 is
    A. 90/330
    B. 120/330
    C. 120/360
    D. 90/360

    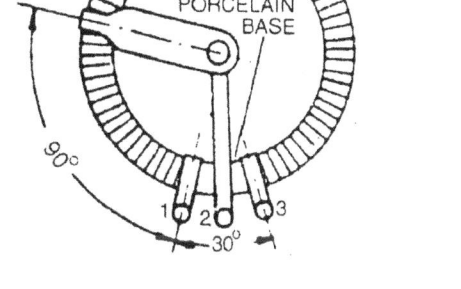

15. The instrument shown is properly connected to measure
    A. a.c. amperes
    B. d.c. amperes
    C. a.c. volts
    D. d.c. volts

    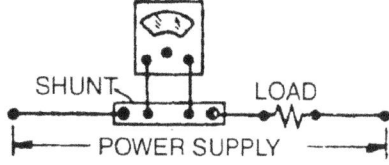

16. The reading of the voltmeter should be
    A. 50
    B. 10
    C. 5
    D. 0

    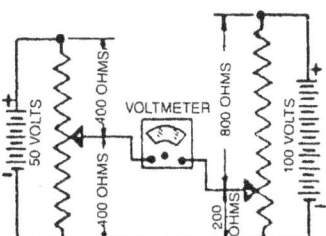

17. If each of the four 90 conduit elbows has the dimensions shown, the distance S is
    A. 20"
    B. 22"
    C. 24"
    D. 26"

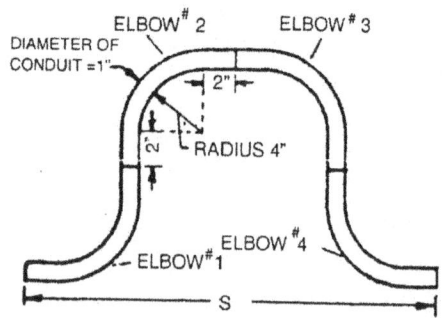

18. The range of both voltmeters shown is 0-300 volts. In this case, the a.c. meter will indicate the correct voltage and the d.c. meter will indicate
    A. zero
    B. a few volts too high
    C. a few volts too low
    D. the correct voltage

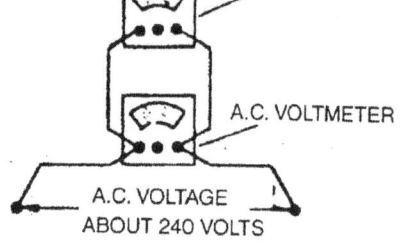

19. The reading on the meter scale shown is
    A. 46
    B. 52
    C. 64
    D. 72

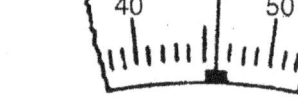

20. The width of the pole piece, in inches, is
    A. 1 7/6
    B. 1 5/16
    C. 11/8
    D. 5 5/16

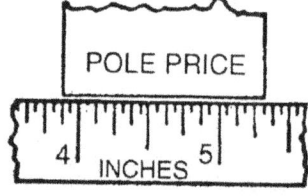

21. The wires in the right-hand junction box are to be spliced so that the switch will control both lighting fixtures and the fixtures will be connected in parallel. The wires to be spliced, in accordance with good wiring practice, are

    A. 1 to 4, 2 to 6
       3 to both 5 and 7
    B. 1 to 6, 2 to 5,
       3 to both 4 and 7
    C. 1 to 7, 2 to both
       5 and 6, 3 to 4
    D. 1 to 5, 2 to both
       6 and 7, 3 to 4

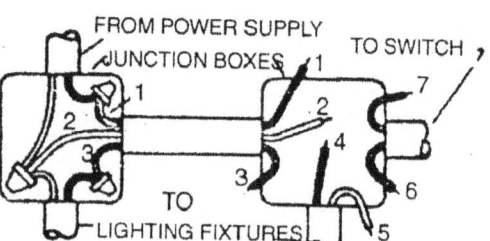

22. The sketch shows four standard rigid electrical conduit sizes in cross-section. The one which is nominal 1/2-inch conduit is No.
    A. 1
    B. 2
    C. 3
    D. 4

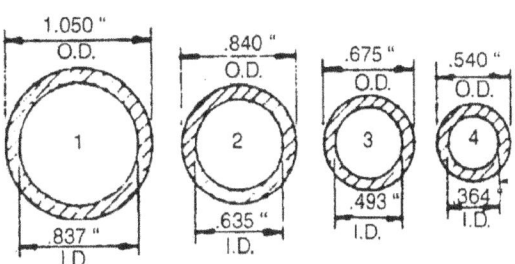

23. The device shown is one element of an iron grid-resistor. Such a large resistor would logically be used when the
    A. resistance required is very high
    B. voltage across it is very high
    C. resistor is to be used outdoors
    D. resistor must carry large currents

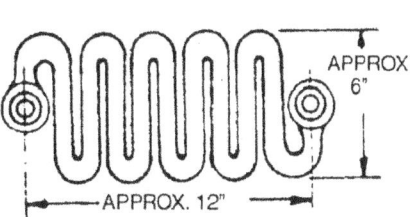

24. The purpose of the auxiliary blade on the knife switch shown is to
    A. delay the opening of the circuit when the handle is pulled open
    B. cut down arcing by opening the circuit quickly
    C. retain the blades in place
    D. increase the capacity of the switch

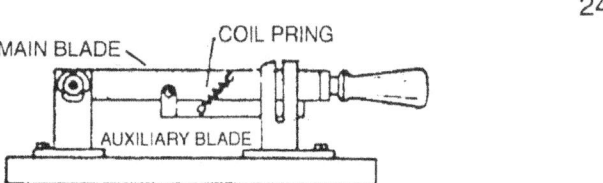

25. The sketch shows a head-on view of a three-pronged plug intended for use with portable electrical tools. Considering the danger of shock when using such tools, it is evident that the function of the U-shaped prong is to

    A. insure that the other two prongs enter the outlet with the proper polarity
    B. provide a half-voltage connection when doing light work
    C. prevent accidental pulling of the plug from the outlet
    D. connect the metallic shell of the tool motor to ground

26. Of the following, the poorest conductor of electricity is

    A. carbon   B. aluminum
    C. copper   D. silver

27. Condensers are sometimes connected across relay contacts that make and break frequently. The purpose of using a condenser in this manner is to

    A. store a charge for the next operation
    B. reduce arcing at the relay contacts
    C. reduce the energy required for relay operation
    D. make the relay quick acting

28. Certain vacuum tubes have four elements inside the glass envelope; namely, a heater, a cathode, a grid, and a plate. In most vacuum tube circuits, the highest "plus" d.c. voltage is applied to the

   A. plate   B. grid   C. cathode   D. heater

29. A fuse puller is used in replacing

   A. plug fuses
   B. link fuses
   C. ribbon fuses
   D. cartridge fuses

30. The National Electrical Code requires that conduit must be continuous from outlet to outlet, must be mechanically and electrically connected to all fittings, and must be suitably grounded. The reason for having the conduit electrically continuous and grounded is to

   A. provide a metallic return conductor
   B. shield the wires inside the conduit from external magnetic fields
   C. make it easy to test wiring connections
   D. prevent electrical shock which might otherwise result from contact with the conduit

31. If a fellow helper has frequent accidents, it is most likely that he is

   A. not physically strong enough to do the job
   B. simply one of those persons who is unlucky
   C. not paying enough attention to safe work habits
   D. trying too hard

32. When a certain motor is started up, the incandescent lights fed from the same circuit dim down somewhat and then return to approximately normal brightness as the motor comes up to speed. This definitely shows that the

   A. starting current of the motor is larger than the running current
   B. insulation of the circuit wiring is worn
   C. circuit fuse is not making good contact
   D. incandescent lamps are too large for the circuit

33. One type of electric motor tends to "run away" if it is not always connected to its load. This motor is the

   A. d.c. series
   B. d.c. shunt
   C. a.c. induction
   D. a.c. synchronous

34. The resistance of 1000 feet of #10 A.W.G. wire is approximately 1 ohm. If the resistance of a coil of #10 A.W.G. wire is 1.19 ohms, the length of wire in the coil is nearest to ____ feet.

   A. 1109   B. 1119   C. 1190   D. 1199

35. The proper tool with which to make a 3/4" diameter hole in a wooden cable cleat is the

   A. reamer   B. countersink   C. auger   D. keyhole saw

36. If three resistors of 175 ohms, 75 ohms, and 17 ohms respectively, are connected in parallel, the combined resistance will be

   A. greater than 175 ohms
   B. between 175 ohms and 75 ohms
   C. between 75 ohms and 17 ohms
   D. less than 17 ohms

37. To determine which wire of a two-wire 120-volt a.c. line is the grounded wire, one correct procedure is to

   A. connect a center-zero voltmeter across the line and note the direction of movement of the pointer
   B. quickly touch each line wire in turn to a cold-water pipe
   C. connect one lead of a test lamp to the conduit, and test each side of the line with the other lead
   D. thrust the two line wires about an inch apart into a slice of raw potato and watch for discoloration

37._____

38. While working on a certain track between stations in the subway, a helper notices a man standing on an adjacent track and suspects from the man's actions that he may have no business being there. The most reasonable procedure would be to

   A. continue working and ignore the man
   B. order the man to get off the tracks immediately
   C. ask the man what business he has being there
   D. hold the man for questioning by police

38._____

39. With respect to safety of personnel, it is probably *LEAST* important to

   A. have a place for each tool and put each tool in its place at the end of each day
   B. place each tool where it cannot fall down and hurt anyone when working on a job
   C. coat each tool with grease at the end of each day to prevent rust
   D. inspect carefully all tools to be used before beginning the day's work

39._____

40. The incoming power supply is usually wired to the "break" jaws rather than to the blades of an exposed knife switch. This practice is followed so that the

   A. blades will be dead when the switch is open
   B. arc will break quickly when the switch is opened
   C. fuses can be replaced without opening the switch
   D. switch can be closed with a minimum of arcing

40._____

41. The speed of a d.c. shunt motor is generally regulated by means of a

   A. switch for reversal of the armature supply
   B. source of variable supply voltage
   C. variable resistance in the armature circuit
   D. rheostat in the field circuit

41._____

42. With respect to fluorescent lamps it is correct to say that

   A. the filaments seldom burn out
   B. they are considerably easier to handle than incandescent lamps
   C. their efficiency is less than the efficiency of incandescent lamps
   D. the starters and the lamps must be replaced at the same time

42._____

43. If your maintainer asked you to bring the tools needed to install a metal first-aid cabinet on a concrete wall, you would need, besides a hammer and a screw driver, a

   A. hack saw   B. star drill
   C. cold chisel   D. socket wrench

43._____

44. A 6-32 machine screw necessarily differs from an 8-32 screw in

   A. length
   B. number of threads per inch
   C. shape of head
   D. diameter

45. A conduit coupling is sometimes tightened by using a strap wrench rather than by using a Stillson wrench.
    The strap wrench is used when it is important to avoid

   A. crushing the conduit
   B. stripping the pipe threads
   C. bending the conduit
   D. damaging the outside finish

46. As you are coming up the subway steps leading to the street, an incoming passenger asks you for traveling directions to a particular destination. If you are not sure of the exact directions, your best course is to

   A. give him the best directions you know
   B. tell him to ask a conductor when he is on the train
   C. tell him to ask the man in the change booth
   D. suggest that he should ask another passenger

47. An electrician's knife should NOT be used to

   A. cut copper wires
   B. remove rubber insulation
   C. cut friction tape
   D. sharpen pencils

48. A test lamp using an ordinary lamp bulb is commonly used to test

   A. for polarity of a d.c. power supply
   B. whether a power supply is a.c. or d.c.
   C. whether a circuit is overloaded
   D. for grounds on 120-volt circuits

49. The filament of a regular incandescent electric lamp is usually made of

   A. tungsten   B. carbon   C. nickel   D. iron

50. After No. 2 A.W.G., the next smaller copper wire or cable size is No.

   A. 0   B. 1   C. 3   D. 4

KEY (CORRECT ANSWERS)

1. C	11. D	21. B	31. C	41. D
2. C	12. A	22. B	32. A	42. A
3. D	13. C	23. D	33. A	43. B
4. C	14. A	24. B	34. C	44. D
5. A	15. B	25. D	35. C	45. D
6. D	16. C	26. A	36. D	46. C
7. C	17. D	27. B	37. C	47. A
8. C	18. A	28. A	38. C	48. D
9. A	19. C	29. D	39. C	49. A
10. B	20. A	30. D	40. A	50. C

EXAMINATION SECTION
TEST 1

DIRECTIONS: Each question or incomplete statement is followed by several suggested answers or completions. Select the one that *BEST* answers the question or completes the statement. *PRINT THE LETTER OF THE CORRECT ANSWER IN THE SPACE AT THE RIGHT.*

1. The letters S.P.S.T. frequently found on wiring plans refer to a type of 1._____

    A. cable   B. switch   C. fuse   D. motor

2. Renewable fuses differ from ordinary fuses in that 2._____

    A. they can carry higher overloads
    B. burned out fuses can be located more easily
    C. burned out fuse elements can be readily replaced
    D. they can be used on higher voltages

3. When a maintainer reports a minor trouble orally to his foreman, the most important information the foreman would require from the maintainer would be the 3._____

    A. type of trouble and its exact location
    B. names of all men with him when he discovered the trouble
    C. exact time the trouble was discovered
    D. work he was doing when he noted the trouble

4. A helper can most quickly make himself useful on the job if he 4._____

    A. asks questions of his foreman at every opportunity
    B. continually suggests changes in work procedures to the maintainer
    C. listens carefully to instructions and carries them out
    D. insists on doing all heavy lifting himself

5. After No. 10 A.W.G., the next smaller copper wire size in common use is No. 5._____

    A. 8   B. 9   C. 11   D. 12

6. The best of the following tools to use for cutting off a piece of single-conductor #6 rubber insulated lead covered cable is a 6._____

    A. pair of electrician's pliers
    B. hacksaw
    C. hammer and cold chisel
    D. lead knife

7. Transit employees whose work requires them to enter upon the tracks in the subway are cautioned not to wear loose fitting clothing. The most important reason for this caution is that loose fitting clothing may 7._____

    A. interfere when they are using heavy tools
    B. catch on some projection of a passing train
    C. give insufficient protection against dust
    D. tear more easily than snug fitting clothing

8. It would *NOT* be good practice to tighten a one-inch hexagon nut with

   A. a monkey wrench
   B. a one-inch fixed open end wrench
   C. an adjustable open-end wrench
   D. a Stillson wrench

9. Lock washers are used principally with

   A. machine screws B. wood screws
   C. self-tapping screws D. lag screws

10. Toggle bolts are most appropriate for use to fasten conduit clamps to a

    A. steel column B. concrete wall
    C. hollow tile wall D. brick wall

11. If a 10-24 by 3/4" machine screw is not available, the screw which could be most easily modified to use in an emergency is a

    A. 10-24 by 1/2" B. 12-24 by 3/4"
    C. 10-24 by 1 1/2" D. 8-24 by 3/4"

12. Lighting in many of the subway cars is provided by 22 lamps all connected in a single series circuit which is fed from the third rail at 600 volts. The voltage rating of each individual lamp in the series must be approximately

    A. 600 volts B. 120 volts
    C. 30 volts D. 22 volts

13. In attempting to revive a person who has stopped breathing after receiving an electric shock, it is most important to

    A. start artificial respiration immediately
    B. wrap the victim in a blanket
    C. massage the ankles and wrists
    D. force the victim to swallow a stimulant

14. After pulling the fuse of a 600-volt circuit, and before starting the work of connecting additional equipment to the circuit, the most important safety precaution to take is to

    A. examine the condition of the fuse
    B. disconnect all load from the circuit
    C. check that all tools have insulated handles
    D. test to make sure the circuit is dead

15. The most practical way to determine in the field if a large coil of #14 wire has the required length for a given job is to

    A. weigh the coil and compare with a new 1000-foot coil
    B. measure the electrical resistance and compare with a 1000-foot coil
    C. measure the length of one turn and multiply by the number of turns
    D. unwind the coil and lay the wire alongside the conduit before pulling it in

16. Maintainers of the transit system are required to report defective equipment to their superiors, even when the maintenance of the particular equipment is handled entirely by another bureau. The purpose of this rule is to

    A. fix responsibility
    B. discourage slackers
    C. encourage alertness
    D. prevent accidents

16.____

17. A standard pipe thread differs from a standard screw thread in that the pipe thread

    A. is tapered
    B. is deeper
    C. requires no lubrication when cutting
    D. has the same pitch for any diameter of pipe

17.____

18. The material which is *LEAST* likely to be found in use as the outer covering of rubber insulated wires or cables is

    A. cotton
    B. varnished cambric
    C. lead
    D. neoprene

18.____

19. In measuring to determine the size of a stranded insulated conductor, the proper place to use the wire gauge is on

    A. the insulation
    B. the outer covering
    C. the stranded conductor
    D. one strand of the conductor

19.____

20. Rubber insulation on an electrical conductor would most quickly be damaged by continuous contact with

    A. acid   B. water   C. oil   D. alkali

20.____

21. If a fuse clip becomes hot under normal circuit load, the most probable cause is that the

    A. clip makes poor contact with the fuse ferrule
    B. circuit wires are too small
    C. current rating of the fuse is too high
    D. voltage rating of the fuse is too low

21.____

22. If the input to a 10 to 1 step-down transformer is 15 amperes at 2400 volts, the secondary output would be nearest to

    A. 1.5 amperes at 24,000 volts
    B. 150 amperes at 240 volts
    C. 1.5 amperes at 240 volts
    D. 150 amperes at 24,000 volts

22.____

23. The resistance of a copper wire to the flow of electricity

    A. increases as the diameter of the wire increases
    B. decreases as the diameter of the wire decreases
    C. decreases as the length of the wire increases
    D. increases as the length of the wire increases

23.____

24. Where galvanized steel conduit is used, the primary purpose of the galvanizing is to   24.____

   A. increase mechanical strength
   B. retard rusting
   C. provide a good surface for painting
   D. provide good electrical contact for grounding

25. The lamps used for station and tunnel lighting in the subways are generally operated at   25.____
slightly less than their rated voltage. The logical reason for this is to

   A. prevent overloading of circuits
   B. increase the life of the lamps
   C. decrease glare
   D. obtain a more even distribution of light

26. The correct method of measuring the power taken by an a.c. electric motor is to use a   26.____

   A. wattmeter
   B. voltmeter and an ammeter
   C. power factor meter
   D. tachometer

27. Assume that you have been asked to get the tools for a maintainer to use in taking down   27.____
a run of exposed conduit (including outlet boxes) from its installed location on the surface
of a concrete wall. The combination of tools which would probably prove most useful
would be a

   A. Stillson wrench, a box wrench, and a hack saw
   B. hack saw, a screw driver, and an adjustable open-end wrench
   C. screw driver, an adjustable open-end wrench, and a Stillson wrench
   D. screw driver, a hammer, and a box wrench

Questions 28 - 37.
Questions 28 through 37 refer to the use of the tools shown on the next page. Read the item and, for the operation given, select the proper tool to be used from those shown. PRINT, in the correspondingly numbered item space at the right, the letter given below your selected tool.

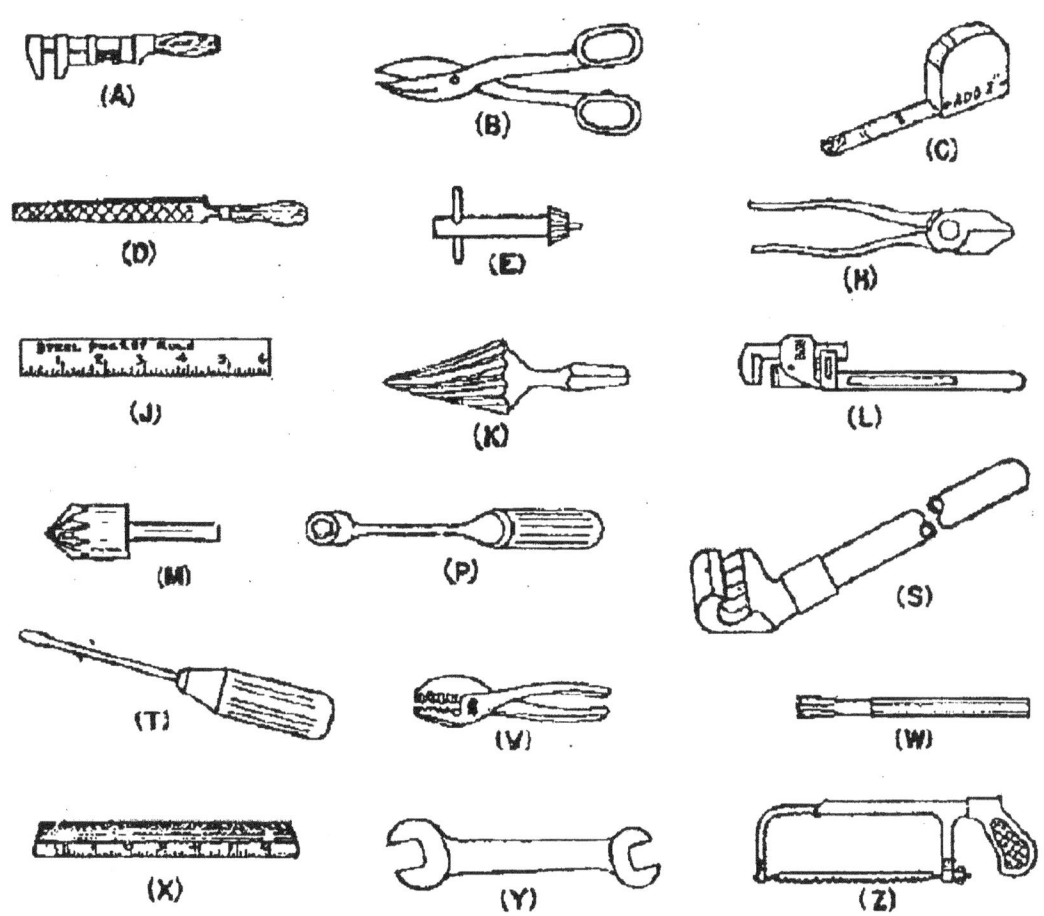

28. Loosening the nut holding a wire on a stud terminal. 28._____

29. Removing burrs from the inner edge of conduit after cutting it. 29._____

30. Measuring the distance between exposed terminals on a low-voltage switchboard which is alive. 30._____

31. Loosening a coupling which is tight on the end of a piece of conduit. 31._____

32. Tightening the chuck on an electric drill. 32._____

33. Tightening a 3/4 inch conduit bushing inside an outlet box. 33._____

34. Skinning a no. 14 A.W.G. rubber insulated wire. 34._____

35. Cutting off part of a brass machine screw which is too long. 35._____

36. Prying off a rubber gasket that is stuck to the inside of the cover that has been taken off a watertight pull box. 36._____

37. Making a hole for a lead anchor in a concrete wall. 37._____

38. The sketch which correctly represents the cross-section of a standard stranded copper con- ductor is

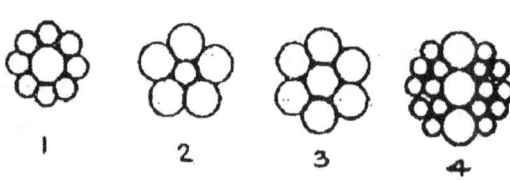

A. 1   B. 2   C. 3   D. 4

39. The reading of the voltmeter should be

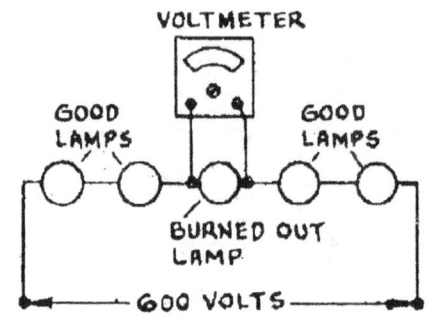

A. 600   B. 300   C. 120   D. zero

40. If the voltage of each of the dry cells shown is 1.5 volts, the voltage between X and Y is
    A. 3
    B. 6
    C. 9
    D. 12

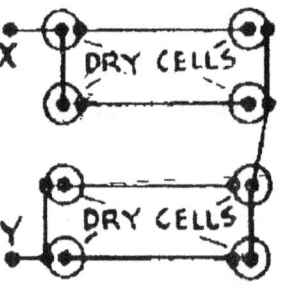

41. In accordance with the voltages shown, the power supply must be
    A. three-wire d.c.
    B. three-phase a.c.
    C. two-phase a.c.
    D. single-phase a.c.

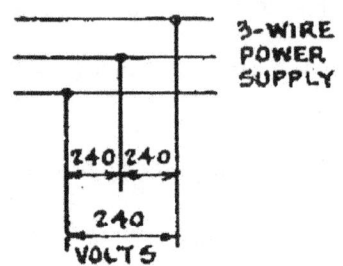

42. Meter 1 is
    A. an ammeter
    B. a frequency meter
    C. a wattmeter
    D. a voltmeter

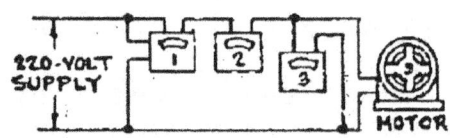

43. The insulator shown is a
    A. pin type insulator
    B. strain insulator
    C. suspension type insulator
    D. insulating bushing

44. The two coils are wound in the directions indicated and both coils have exactly the same number of turns. When the switch is closed, the north pole of the permanent magnet will be
    A. repelled by both the left-hand and right-hand cores
    B. attracted by both the left-hand and right-hand cores
    C. attracted by the left-hand core and repelled by the right-hand core
    D. repelled by the left-hand core and attracted by the right-hand core

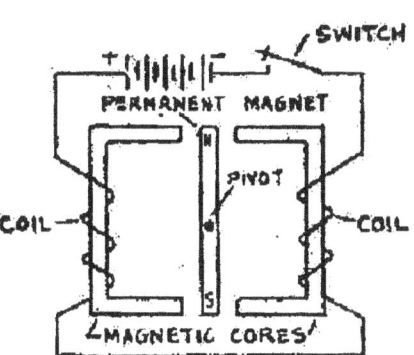

45. Regardless of the battery voltage, it is clear that the smallest current is in the resistor having a resistance of
    A. 200 ohms
    B. 300 ohms
    C. 400 ohms
    D. 500 ohms

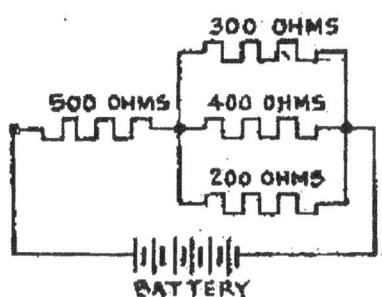

46. The five lamps shown are each rated at 120-volts 60-watts. If all are good lamps, lamp no. 5 will be
    A. much brighter than normal
    B. about its normal brightness
    C. much dimmer than normal
    D. completely dark

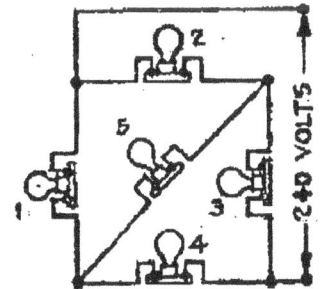

47. If the voltmeter reads 34 volts, the circuit voltage is about
    A. 68
    B. 85
    C. 102
    D. 119

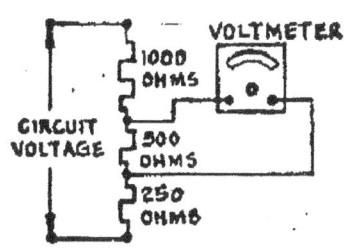

48. If the voltage of the supply is 120 volts, the readings of the voltmeter should be
    A. 60 volts on each meter
    B. 120 volts on each meter
    C. 80 volts on meter #1 and 40 volts on meter #2
    D. 80 volts on meter #2 and 40 volts on meter #1

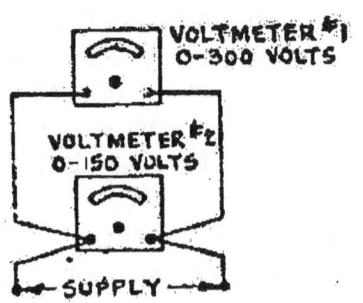

48.____

49. The sketch shows the four resistance dials and the multiplying dial of a resistance bridge. The four resistance dials can be set to any value of resistance up to 10,000 ohms, and the multiplier can be set at any of the nine points shown. In their present positions, the five pointers indicate a reading of
    A. 13.60
    B. 136,000
    C. 130,600
    D. 13.06

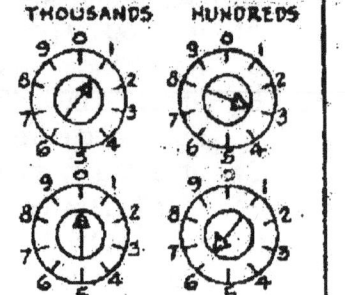
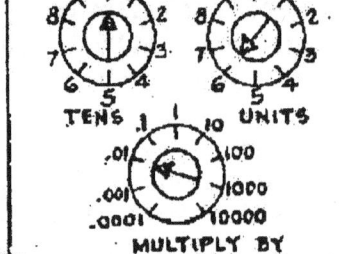

49.____

50. The indication on the meter scale is
    A. 266
    B. 258
    C. 253
    D. 251.5

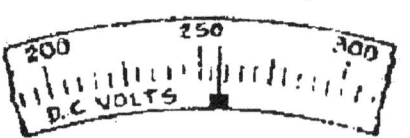

50.____

KEY (CORRECT ANSWERS)

1. B	11. C	21. A	31. L	41. B
2. C	12. C	22. B	32. E	42. C
3. A	13. A	23. D	33. V	43. A
4. C	14. D	24. B	34. H	44. A
5. D	15. C	25. B	35. H	45. C
6. B	16. D	26. A	36. T	46. D
7. B	17. A	27. C	37. W	47. D
8. D	18. B	28. P	38. C	48. B
9. A	19. D	29. K	39. A	49. D
10. C	20. C	30. X	40. B	50. B

TEST 2

DIRECTIONS: Each question or incomplete statement is followed by several suggested answers or completions. Select the one that BEST answers the question or completes the statement. *PRINT THE LETTER OF THE CORRECT ANSWER IN THE SPACE AT THE RIGHT.*

1. The reading of the kilowatt-hour meter is
   A. 7972
   B. 2786
   C. 1786
   D. 6872

   1._____

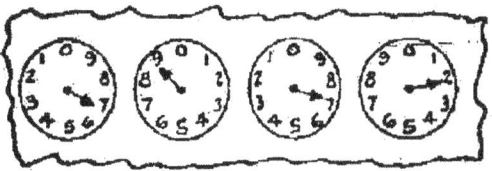

2. The reading shown on the micrometer is
   A. 0.203
   B. 0.222
   C. 0.228
   D. 0.247

   2._____

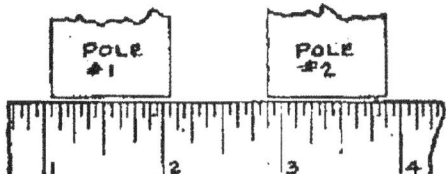

3. The center to center distance between the two poles is

   A. $\dfrac{11"}{16}$

   B. $1\dfrac{1"}{16}$

   C. $1\dfrac{11"}{16}$

   D. $1\dfrac{13"}{16}$

   3._____

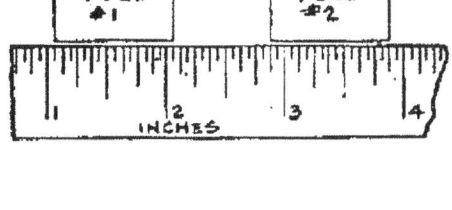

4. The outlet which will accept the plug is
   A. 1
   B. 2
   C. 3
   D. 4

   4._____

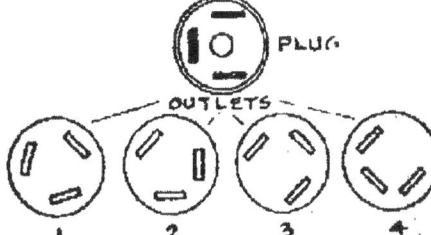

5. The double-pole double-throw switch which is properly connected as a reversing switch is
   A. 1
   B. 2
   C. 3
   D. 4

   5._____

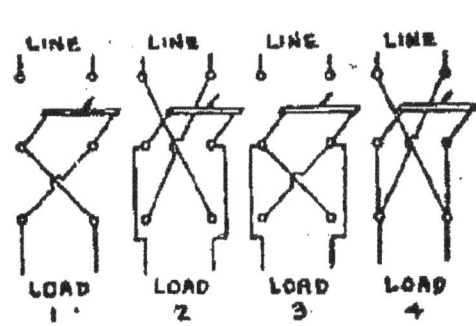

6. The standard coupling for rigid electrical conduit is
   A. 1
   B. 2
   C. 3
   D. 4

7. The shape of nut most commonly used on electrical terminals is
   A. 1
   B. 2
   C. 3
   D. 4

8. The stove bolt is
   A. 1
   B. 2
   C. 3
   D. 4

Questions 9 - 14.
Questions 9 through 14 refer to the figures on the following page.
Each item gives the proper figure to use with that item.

9. Referring to Figure 1, if the 500-ohm resistor becomes open circuited, the reading of the ammeter will probably
   A. remain unchanged
   B. decrease
   C. increase
   D. drop to zero

10. The total equivalent resistance in ohms between points X and Y in Figure 2 is
    A. 3   B. 5   C. 15   D. 45

11. The reading of the voltmeter in Figure 3 should be
    A. 150   B. 100   C. 50   D. zero

12. In Figure 4, if switch 1 only is closed the reading of the voltmeter will
    A. increase
    B. decrease, but not to zero
    C. remain unchanged
    D. become zero

13. In Figure 4, if switch 2 only is closed the reading of the voltmeter will
    A. increase
    B. decrease, but not to zero
    C. remain unchanged
    D. become zero

14. In Figure 4, if switch 3 only is closed the reading of the voltmeter will
    A. increase
    B. decrease, but not to zero
    C. remain unchanged
    D. become zero

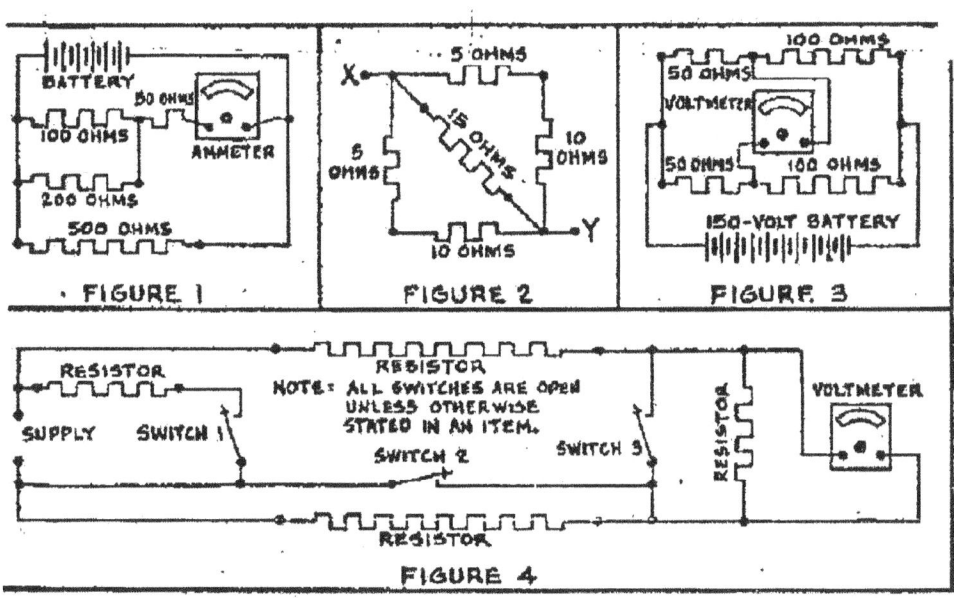

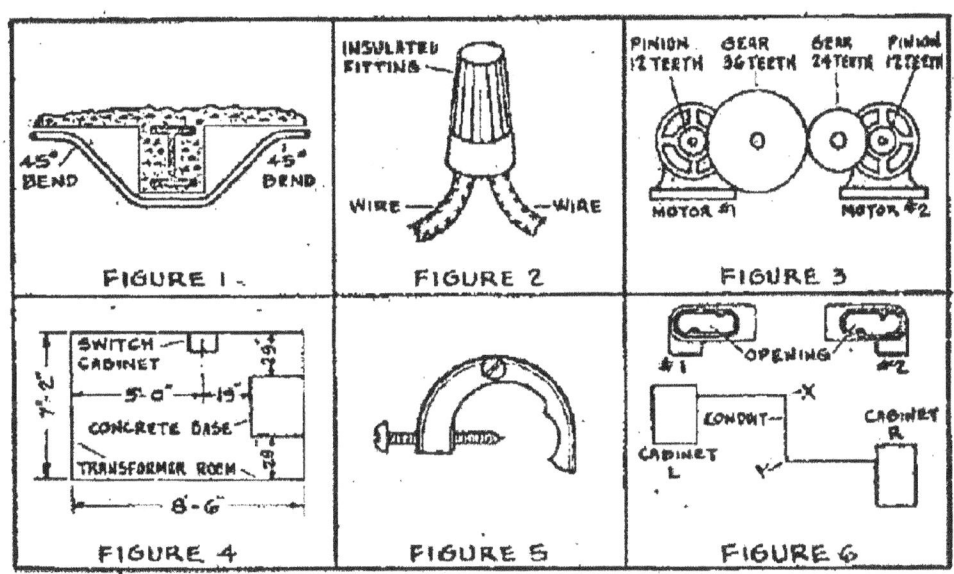

Questions 15 - 20.
Questions 15 through 20 refer to the figures above. Each item gives the proper figure to use with that item.

15. When a wire is pulled into the conduit in Figure 1, it must go around bends amounting to a total of   15._____

    A. 0°   B. 90°   C. 180°   D. 360°

16. Wires are often spliced by the use of a fitting like the one shown in Figure 2. The use of this fitting does away with the need for   16._____

    A. skinning   B. cleaning
    C. twisting   D. soldering

17. The two identical motors in Figure 3 are connected to the same power supply and are wired so that they normally tend to turn in the same direction. When the power is turned on

    A. the motors will stall
    B. both motors will turn at normal speed in the same direction
    C. motor #1 will turn in its normal direction driving motor #2 backwards
    D. motor #2 will turn in its normal direction driving motor #1 backwards

18. The dimensions of the concrete base shown in Figure 4 are

    A. 14" x 28"
    B. 23" x 28"
    C. 23" x 29"
    D. 14" x 29"

19. The device shown in Figure 5 is a

    A. C-clamp
    B. test clip
    C. battery connector
    D. ground clamp

20. Figure 6 shows two types of conduit fitting (#1 and #2) used as pull boxes at sharp bends in conduit runs. The figure also shows the layout of a conduit run on the wall between cabinets L and R. If wire is to be pulled into the conduit starting at cabinet L, and the wire is to be continuous without a splice from cabinet L to cabinet R, the best choice of fittings is to have a

    A. #1 at corner X and a #2 at corner Y
    B. #2 at both corners X and Y
    C. #1 at both corners X and Y
    D. #2 at corner X and a #1 at corner Y

21. Checking a piece of rigid electrical conduit with a steel scale, you measure the inside diameter as 1 1/16" and the outside diameter as 1 5/16". The nominal size of this conduit is

    A. 3/4" B. 1" C. C 1 1/4" D. D 1 1/2"

22. Of the following, it would be most difficult to solder a copper wire to a metal plate made of

    A. copper B. brass C. iron D. tin

23. After a piece of rigid conduit has been cut. to length, it is most important to

    A. ream the inside edge to prevent injury to wires
    B. file the end flat to make an accurate fit
    C. coat the cut surface with red lead to prevent rust
    D. file the outside edge to a taper for ease in threading

24. When lamps on the transit system are installed at less than 7 ft. 6 in. from the floor, they are provided with lamp guards. The purpose of guards in such cases is most likely to

    A. reduce glare
    B. prevent accidental burning of passengers
    C. minimize lamp breakage
    D. discourage lamp thefts

25. Rigid conduit is generally secured to sheet metal outlet boxes by means of

    A. threadless couplings
    B. box connectors
    C. locknuts and bushings
    D. conduit clamps

26. According to generally recommended practice, helper Richard Roe answering the telephone at the Undercliff Ave. signal section headquarters would do best to say

    A. "Hello, this is Undercliff Ave., Roe speaking."
    B. "This is Roe, -Signal Section."
    C. "Roe, Signal Section, -Who's calling?"
    D. "Signal Section, Undercliff Ave., Roe speaking."

27. While a certain d.c. shunt motor is driving a light load, part of the field winding becomes short circuited. The motor will most likely

    A. increase its speed
    B. decrease its speed
    C. remain at the same speed
    D. come to a stop

28. The circumference of a circle is given by the formula $C = 2\pi R$, where C is the circumference, R is the radius, and π is approximately 3 1/7. The circumference of an oil drum having a diameter of one foot and nine inches is therefore about

    A. 132 inches
    B. 66 inches
    C. 33 inches
    D. 17 inches

29. Each time a certain electric heater is turned on, the incandescent lights connected to the same branch circuit become dimmer and when the heater is turned off the lamps become brighter. The factor which probably contributes most to this effect is the

    A. voltage of the circuit
    B. size of the circuit fuse
    C. current taken by the lamps
    D. size of the circuit conductors

30. Comparing the shunt field winding with the series field winding of a compound d.c. motor, it would be correct to say that the shunt field winding has

    A. more turns but the lower resistance
    B. more turns and the higher resistance
    C. fewer turns and the lower resistance
    D. fewer turns but the higher resistance

Questions 31 - 37.
Questions 31 through 37 are based on the motor inspection instructions given below. Read these instructions carefully before answering these questions.

GENERAL INSTRUCTIONS FOR WEEKLY MOTOR INSPECTION

Inspect each motor to see if there is any unusual amount of dust or chips on or near it, and to see if there is anything left lying about which might interfere with the free running or ventilation of the motor. Check lubrication in accordance with standard instructions for the type of motor. At the same time, take notice of any unusual noise or odor for evidence of excessive wear or overloading; feel bearing housings for heat and vibration. Inspect the commutator of each d.c. motor for discoloration, dirt, and uneven wear; look for sparking at the brushes while the motor is running.

Any minor defect should be corrected on the spot as soon as it is discovered, and the proper report made to your superior of the action taken. Any major defect that is found should be reported promptly to your superior so that it can be corrected before the damage becomes too great to be repaired.

31. One sure sign that there has been sparking at the brushes of a stopped d.c. motor would be

    A. the odor of hot rubber insulation
    B. hot bearings
    C. grooves worn around the commutator
    D. pits on the commutator surface

32. A common way of reducing the chances of uneven commutator wear is to

    A. use brushes of different hardness
    B. allow some end play in the motor bearings
    C. anneal the commutator after assembly
    D. turn the commutator down frequently

33. Upon entering a pump room in which a motor-driven pump is running, the maintainer detects the odor of hot insulating varnish. This odor indicates that the

    A. varnish has been freshly applied
    B. bearings are poorly lubricated
    C. room is insufficiently ventilated
    D. motor is being overloaded

34. If an unusual amount of dust is found around the base of a motor which is being inspected, the proper procedure to follow is to

    A. take no action but report the motor for further inspection
    B. remove the dust and note the action in your daily report
    C. inspect the bearings for signs of excessive wear
    D. lubricate the motor in accordance with standard instructions

35. If one bearing housing of a running motor feels exceptionally hot but there is no unusual vibration, the most logical conclusion is that the

    A. motor is being overloaded
    B. bearing needs lubrication
    C. shaft has become worn
    D. motor has been running a long time

36. During a weekly inspection, the motor driving a certain drainage pump is found to be unusually noisy when it runs. The starting and stopping of this motor is automatically controlled by a float switch. In order to comply with the above general instructions, the

    A. cause should be investigated and the condition reported promptly to your superior for corrective action
    B. float switch should be adjusted so that the motor will run less frequently
    C. motor should be shut down immediately
    D. bearings should be lubricated in accordance with standard instructions

37. When making a weekly motor inspection you would be LEAST likely to need a

    A. grease gun   B. dust brush
    C. thermometer   D. flashlight

38. The most important reason for using a fuse-puller when removing a cartridge fuse from the fuse clips is to

    A. prevent blowing of the fuse
    B. prevent injury to the fuse element
    C. reduce the chances of personal injury
    D. reduce arcing at the fuse clips

39. A coil of wire wound on an iron core draws exactly 5 amperes when connected across the terminals of a ten-volt storage battery. If this coil is now connected across the ten-volt secondary terminals of an ordinary power transformer, the current drawn will be

    A. less than 5 amperes
    B. more than 5 amperes
    C. exactly 5 amperes
    D. more or less than 5 amperes depending on the frequency

40. Standard iron conduit comes in 10-foot lengths. The number of such lengths required for a run of 23 yards is

    A. 3   B. 4   C. 6   D. 7

41. A revolution counter applied to the end of a rotating shaft reads 100 when a stop-watch is started. It reads 850 when the stop-watch indicates 90 seconds. The average RPM of the shaft is

    A. 8.4   B. 9.4   C. 500   D. 567

42. Motor speeds are generally measured directly in RPM by the use of a

    A. potentiometer   B. manometer
    C. dynamometer   D. tachometer

43. A rule of the transit system is that the system telephones must not be used for personal calls. The most important reason for this rule is that such personal calls

    A. increase telephone maintenance
    B. tie up telephones which may be urgently needed for company business
    C. waste company time
    D. require additional operators

44. To reverse the direction of rotation of a 3-phase motor, it is necessary to 44.____

    A. increase the resistance of the rotor circuit
    B. interchange any two of the three line connections
    C. interchange all three line connections
    D. reverse the polarity of the rotor circuit

45. Mica is commonly used in electrical construction for 45.____

    A. commutator bar separators
    B. switchboard panels
    C. strain insulators
    D. heater cord insulation

46. The rating term "1000 ohms, 10 watts" would generally be applied to a 46.____

    A. heater   B. relay   C. resistor   D. transformer

47. According to the National Electrical Code, the identified (or grounded) conductor of the branch circuit supplying an incandescent lamp socket must be connected to the screw shell. The most likely reason for this requirement is that 47.____

    A. longer lamp life results
    B. the wiring will be kept more nearly uniform
    C. persons are more likely to come in contact with the shell
    D. the shell can carry heavier currents

48. In an installation used to charge a storage battery from a motor-generator you would LEAST expect to find 48.____

    A. a rectifier   B. a rheostat
    C. a voltmeter   D. an ammeter

49. The letters R.I.L.C. are used in identifying 49.____

    A. transformers   B. motors
    C. cables   D. storage batteries

50. Two separate adjacent lamp bulbs are placed behind each colored lens of the train signals alongside the tracks in the subway. The logical reason why two bulbs are used instead of one bulb is to 50.____

    A. permit lower line voltage
    B. increase the light intensity
    C. permit the use of smaller bulbs
    D. keep the signal lighted in case one bulb fails

KEY (CORRECT ANSWERS)

1. D	11. D	21. B	31. D	41. C
2. B	12. C	22. C	32. B	42. D
3. D	13. A	23. A	33. D	43. B
4. C	14. D	24. D	34. B	44. B
5. B	15. C	25. C	35. B	45. A
6. A	16. D	26. D	36. A	46. C
7. B	17. A	27. A	37. C	47. C
8. C	18. B	28. B	38. C	48. A
9. C	19. D	29. D	39. A	49. C
10. B	20. D	30. B	40. D	50. D

EXAMINATION SECTION
TEST 1

DIRECTIONS: Each question or incomplete statement is followed by several suggested answers or completions. Select the one that *BEST* answers the question or completes the statement. *PRINT THE LETTER OF THE CORRECT ANSWER IN THE SPACE AT THE RIGHT.*

1. The core of an electro-magnet is usually

   A. aluminum   B. lead   C. brass   D. iron

2. The purpose of applying artificial respiration to the victim of an electric shock is to

   A. restore blood circulation
   B. avoid excessive loss of blood
   C. keep the victim warm
   D. supply oxygen to the lungs

3. Electrical maintenance workers whose duties require them to be on the tracks in the subway generally work In pairs. Of the following possible reasons for having the two men work together, the *LEAST* likely is that

   A. the tools and equipment are too much for one man to carry
   B. it provides better protection against vandalism
   C. some of the tests and maintenance work require two men
   D. the men can help each other in case of accident

4. A stranded wire is given the same size designation as a solid wire if it has the same

   A. cross-sectional area   B. weight per foot
   C. overall diameter   D. strength

5. Safety regulations prohibit testing even a 20-volt light socket with the fingers to see whether the socket is alive. The main reason for this prohibition is that

   A. such action can become a bad working habit
   B. a 20-volt shock is often fatal
   C. sockets usually have sharp edges
   D. the skin will become less sensitive to higher voltages

6. One advantage of cutting 1" rigid conduit with a hacksaw rather than with a 3-wheel pipe cutter is that

   A. the cut can be made with less exertion
   B. the pipe is not squeezed out of round
   C. less reaming is required after the cut
   D. no vise is needed

7. Rigid conduit used in the subway is galvanized inside and outside. The purpose of the galvanizing is to

   A. protect the wiring by covering rough spots
   B. improve the appearance where the conduit is exposed to view
   C. protect the conduit against corrosion
   D. provide good contact for grounding the conduit

8. If a hacksaw blade becomes worn so that the teeth are no longer properly set, the

   A. blade will tend to bind in the cut
   B. cut will have jagged edges
   C. cutting must all be done on the back stroke
   D. blade will lose its temper

9. If you and another helper are assigned to a hard and tedious job and your co-worker is not doing a reasonable share of the work, your best procedure is to

   A. slow down to his rate
   B. do your share and quit
   C. try to persuade him to do his share
   D. stop and register a complaint with the foreman before continuing

10. The most informative way for John Doe, the helper on duty at the 19th Street Lighting Section headquarters in the subway, to answer the telephone would be to say,

    A. "19th Street, who's calling?"
    B. "John Doe speaking."
    C. "Lighting Section, 19th Street."
    D. "Hello, this is Lighting Section."

11. Assume that the field leads of a large, completely disconnected d.c. motor are not tagged or otherwise marked. You could readily tell the shunt field leads from the series field leads by the

    A. length of the leads
    B. size of wire
    C. thickness of insulation
    D. type of insulation

12. Standard electrician's pliers should NOT be used to

    A. bend thin sheet metal
    B. crush Insulation on wires to be skinned
    C. cut off nail points sticking through a board
    D. hold a wire in position for soldering

13. The device used to change a.c. to d.c. is a

    A. frequency   B. regulator
    C. transformer   D. rectifier

14. The chief advantage of using stranded rather than solid conductors for electrical wiring is that stranded conductors are

    A. more flexible   B. easier to skin
    C. smaller   D. stronger

15. One identifying feature of a squirrel-cage induction motor is that it has no

    A. windings on the stationary part
    B. commutator or slip rings
    C. air gap
    D. iron core in the rotating part

16. It is advisable to close a knife switch firmly and rapidly because then there is less

    A. danger of shock to the operator
    B. chance of making an error
    C. mechanical wear of the contacts
    D. likelihood of arcing

17. If a cartridge fuse is hot to the touch when you remove it to do some maintenance on the circuit, this most probably indicates that the

    A. voltage of the circuit is too high
    B. fuse clips do not make good contact
    C. equipment on the circuit starts and stops frequently
    D. fuse is oversize for the circuit

18. The instrument most commonly used to determine the state of charge of a lead-acid storage battery is the

    A. thermometer
    B. hydrometer
    C. voltmeter
    D. ammeter

19. Smoking is forbidden in rooms housing storage batteries mainly because of the inflammable gas given off when the batteries are being charged. This gas is

    A. hydrogen
    B. carbon monoxide
    C. ammonia
    D. chlorine

20. Rigid conduit must be so installed as to prevent the collection of water in it between outlets. In order to meet this requirement, the conduit should NOT have a

    A. low point between successive outlets
    B. high point between successive outlets
    C. low point at an outlet
    D. high point at an outlet

21. When a test lamp is connected to the two ends of a cartridge fuse on an operating switchboard, the indication in ALL cases will be that this fuse is

    A. blown if the test lamp remains dark
    B. good if the test lamp lights
    C. blown if the test lamp lights
    D. good if the test lamp remains dark

22. If one copper wire has a diameter of 0.128 inch, and another copper wire has a diameter of 0.064 inch, the resistance of 1,000 feet of the first wire compared to the same length of the second wire is

    A. one half
    B. one quarter
    C. double
    D. four times

4 (#1)

23. The area of a circle having a diameter of one inch is closest to

   A. 3/4 square inch
   B. 1 square inch
   C. 1 1/3 square inches
   D. 1 1/2 square inches

24. If the allowable current In a copper bus bar is 1,000 amperes per square inch of cross-section, the width of a standard 1/4" bus bar designed to carry 1500 amperes would be

   A. 2" B. 4" C. 6" D. 8"

25. It is now possible to obtain a 200-watt light-bulb that is as small in all dimensions as the standard 150-watt light-bulb. The principal advantage to users resulting from this reduction in size is that

   A. maintenance electricians can carry many more light-bulbs
   B. two sizes of light-bulbs can be kept in the same storage space
   C. the higher wattage bulb can now fit into certain lighting fixtures
   D. less breakage is apt to occur in handling

26. A carbon brush in a d.c. motor should exert a pressure of about 1 1/2 lbs. per square inch on the commutator.
    A much lighter pressure would be most likely to result in

   A. sparking at the commutator
   B. vibration of the armature
   C. the brush getting out of line
   D. excessive wear of the brush holder

27. The number of watts of heat given off by a resistor is expressed by the formula I^2R. If 10 volts is applied to a 5-ohm resistor, the heat given off will be

   A. 500 watts
   B. 250 watts
   C. 50 watts
   D. 20 watts

Questions 28 - 36.

Questions 28 through 36 in Column I are electrical instruments and devices each of which is represented by one of the symbols in the schematic wiring diagram shown in Column II. For each instrument or device in Column I, select the corresponding symbol from Column II. *PRINT*, in the correspondingly numbered item space at the right, the letter given beside your selected symbol.

5 (#1)

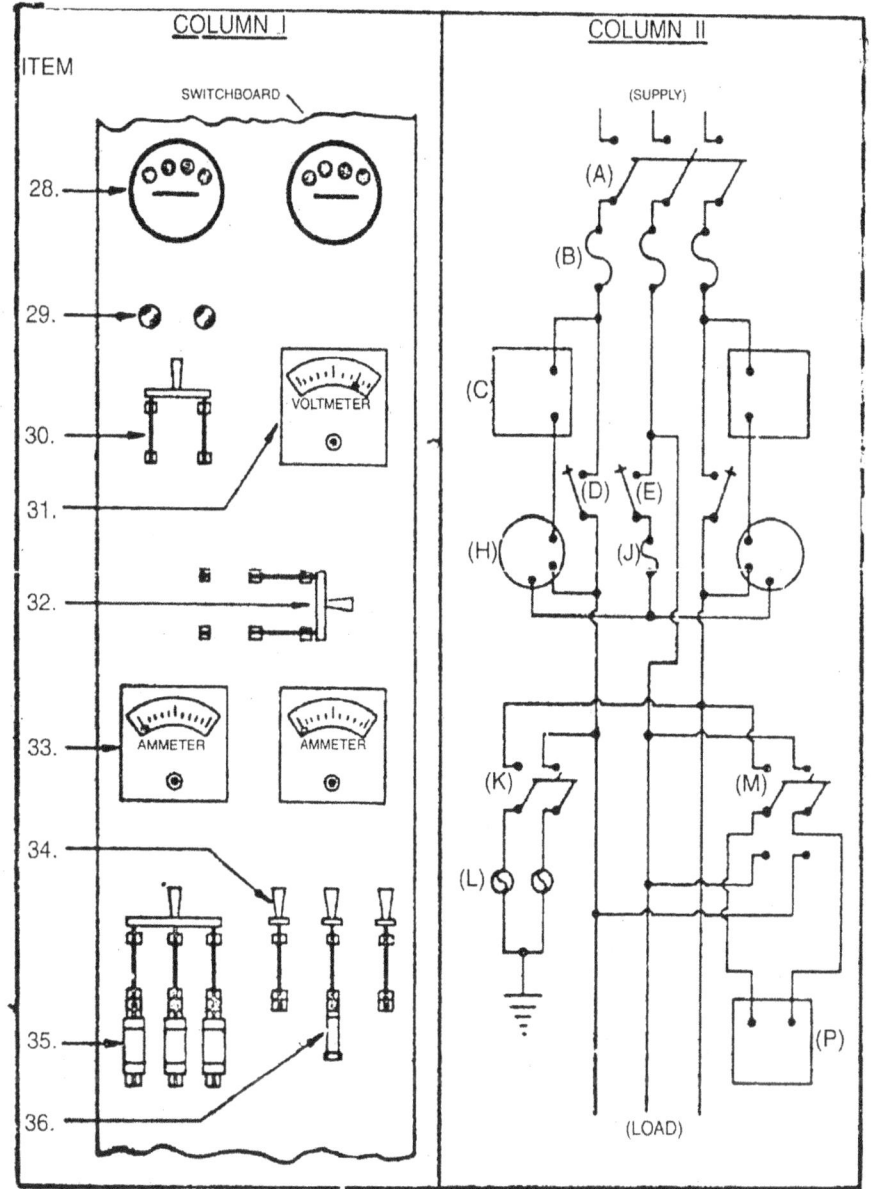

28. ____
29. ____
30. ____
31. ____
32. ____
33. ____
34. ____
35. ____
36. ____

Questions 37 -40.

Questions 37 through 40 in Column I are wiring diagrams of the various positions of two rotary snap-switches each of which is shown in simplified form by one of the circuit diagrams in Column II. For each wiring diagram in Column I, select the simplified circuit diagram from Column II. *PRINT,* in the correspondingly number item space at the right, the letter given beside your selected circuit diagram.

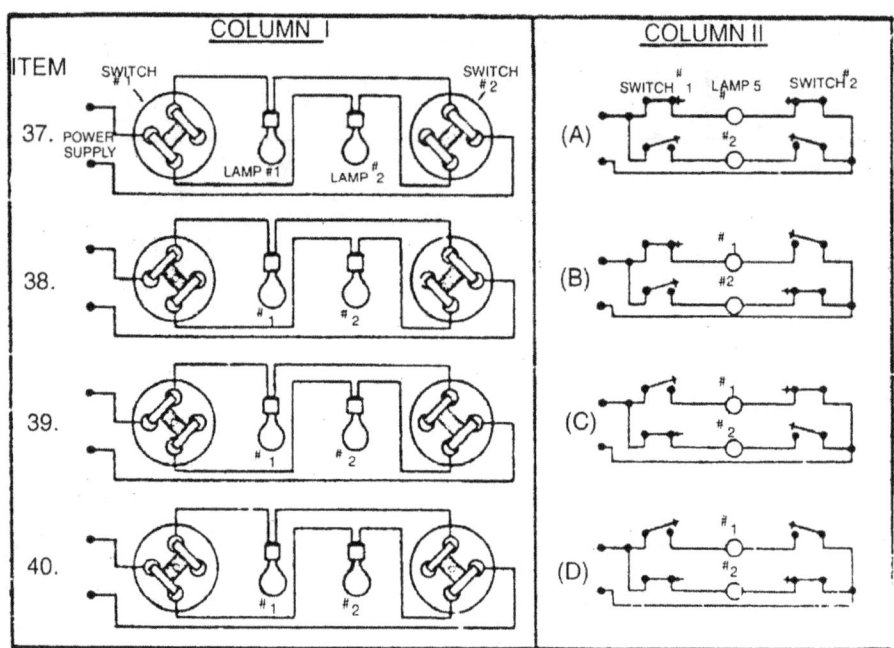

37.____

38.____

39.____

40.____

Questions 41 - 45.

Questions 41 through 45 in Column I are rating-terms each of which is commonly used in association with one of the electrical devices listed in Column II. For each rating-term in Column I, select the most closely associated electrical device from Column II. *PRINT*, in the correspondingly number item space at the right, the letter given beside your selected device.

Column I (rating-terms)		Column II (electrical devices)	
41. 120 watts; 5 ohms	A.	resistor	41._____
42. 120 to 13,800 volts	B.	toggle switch	42._____
43. 120 volts; 100 watts	C.	transformer	43._____
44. 120 volts; 100 amp.-hrs.	D.	light-bulb	44._____
45. 120 volts; 10 amp.	E.	storage battery	45._____

46. Assuming that the same kind of insulating material is used on each of the four copper conductors shown, the one intended for the highest voltage service is number
    A. 1
    B. 2
    C. 3
    D. 4

46._____

47. The convenience outlet that is known as a *POLARIZED* outlet is number
    A. 1
    B. 2
    C. 3
    D. 4

47._____

48. The group of 1 1/2-volt dry cells which is properly connected to deliver 6 volts is number
    A. 1
    B. 2
    C. 3
    D. 4

48._____

49. Each of the four sketches shows the proper schematic connections for one kind of d.c. motor. The one showing the connections for a shunt motor is number
    A. 1
    B. 2
    C. 3
    D. 4

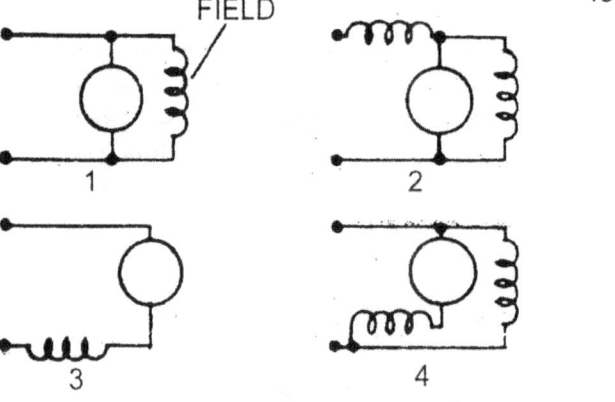

50. The four illustrations show pairs of equal strength permanent magnets on pivots, each magnet being held in the position shown by a mechanical locking device. When they are mechanically unlocked, the magnets which are LEAST likely to change their positions are pair number
    A. 1
    B. 2
    C. 3
    D. 4

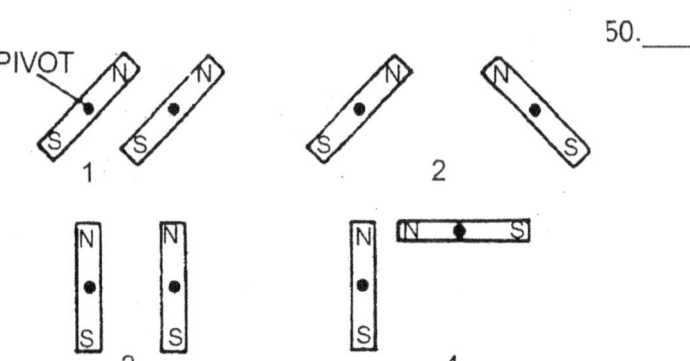

KEY (CORRECT ANSWERS)

1. D	11. B	21. C	31. P	41. A
2. D	12. C	22. B	32. M	42. C
3. B	13. D	23. A	33. C	43. D
4. A	14. A	24. C	34. D	44. E
5. A	15. B	25. C	35. B	45. B
6. C	16. D	26. A	36. J	46. D
7. C	17. B	27. D	37. C	47. A
8. A	18. B	28. H	38. A	48. B
9. C	19. A	29. L	39. B	49. A
10. C	20. A	30. K	40. D	50. C

TEST 2

DIRECTIONS: Each question or incomplete statement is followed by several suggested answers or completions. Select the one that BEST answers the question or completes the statement. PRINT THE LETTER OF THE CORRECT ANSWER IN THE SPACE AT THE RIGHT.

1. If the currents in resistors nos. 1, 2, and 3 are 4.8, 7.5, and 6.2 amperes respectively, then the current (in amperes) in resistor no. 4 is
   A. 1.3
   B. 2.7
   C. 3.5
   D. 6.1

1.____

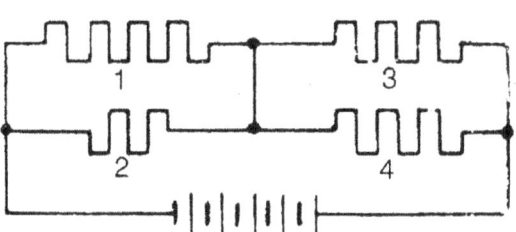

2. If the mercury switch is turned to the horizontal position, the mercury will flow and break the connection between the lead-in wires, thus opening the circuit. By logical reasoning, such a switch would be most useful when

2.____

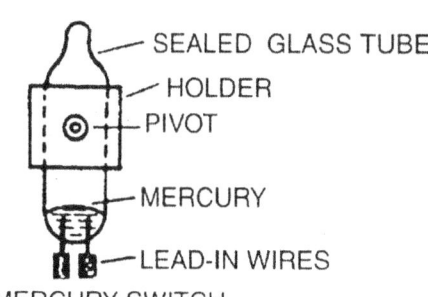

   A. the circuit must be opened quickly
   B. there is likely to be explosive gas near the switch location
   C. there is no restriction on noise
   D. the switch need not be operated often

3. The device shown is clearly intended for use in electrical construction to
   A. support conduit on a wall
   B. join cable to a terminal block
   C. ground a wire to a water pipe
   D. attach a chain-hung lighting fixture to an outlet box

3.____

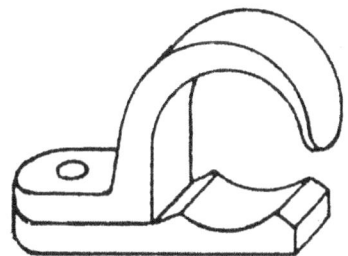

4. The fitting shown is used in electrical construction to
   A. clamp two adjacent junction boxes together
   B. act as a ground clamp for the conduit system
   C. attach flexible metallic conduit to a junction box
   D. protect exposed wires where they pass through a wall

4.____

5. The electrical connector shown would most likely be used in a power plant to connect
   A. two branch cables to a main cable
   B. a single cable to the terminals of two devices
   C. a single cable to a flat bus bar
   D. a round bus bar to a flat one

   5.____

   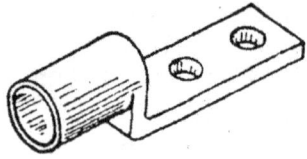

6. If switch S is closed, the resulting change in the ammeter readings will be that
   A. both will increase
   B. both will decrease
   C. #1 will increase and #2 will decrease
   D. #1 will decrease and #2 will increase

   6.____

   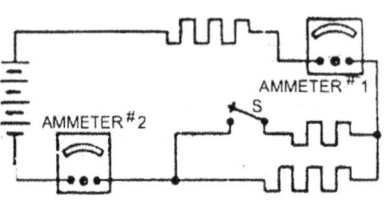

7. If the 10-ohm resistor marked X burns out, the reading of the voltmeter will become
   A. 0
   B. 20
   C. 80
   D. 100

   7.____

   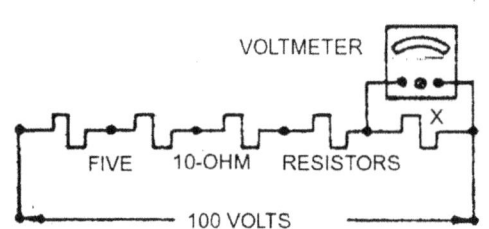

8. The width of the bar, in inches, is
   A. 1 1/8
   B. 1 5/16
   C. 1 7/16
   D. 2 5/16

   8.____

   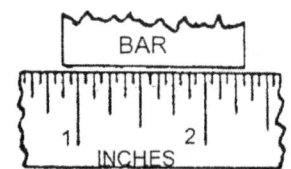

9. The total resistance, in ohms, between points X and Y is
   A. 2.5
   B. 5
   C. 10
   D. 20

   9.____

   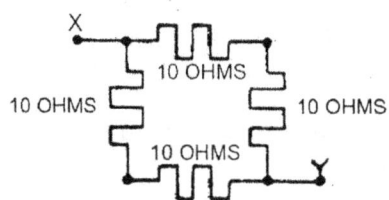

10. The range of both voltmeters shown is 0-150 volts. In this case, the a.c. meter will indicate the correct voltage and the d.c. meter will indicate
    A. the same
    B. a few volts more
    C. a few volts less
    D. zero

    10.____

    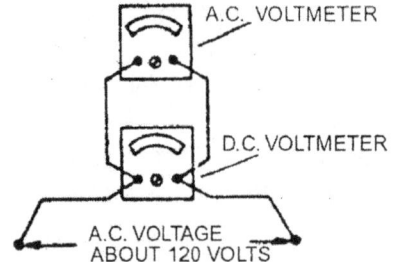

11. The six wires shown are to be properly connected so that the lighting fixture can be controlled by a single-pole on-off switch. The correct connections in accordance with established good practice are

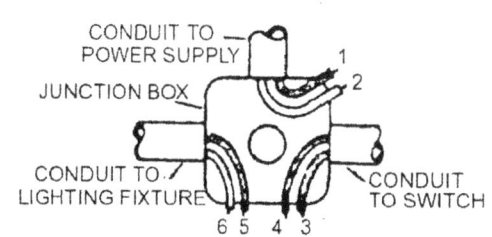

A. 1 to 3 and 5; 2 to 4 and 6
B. 1 to 5; 2 to 3; 4 to 6
C. 1 to 3 and 6; 2 to 4 and 5
D. 1 to 3; 4 to 5; 2 to 6

11.____

12. In the right-angled triangle shown, the angle marked X is
A. 45°
B. 60°
C. 75°
D. 90°

12.____

13. The distance from the top of the desk to the bottom of the lighting fixture is
A. 94"
B. 81"
C. 72"
D. 64"

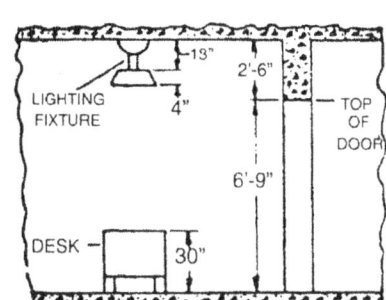

13.____

14. When the movable arm of the uniformly wound resistor is in the position shown, the resistance in ohms between terminals 2 and 3 is
A. 2000
B. 1800
C. 1500
D. 1200

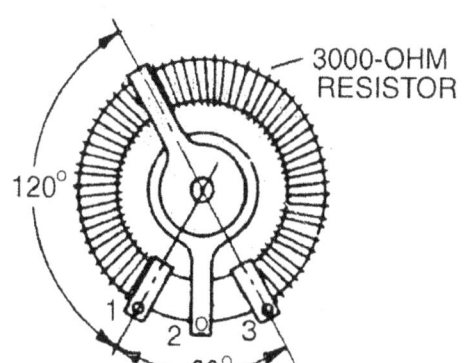

14.____

15. If each of the 19 strands of the conductor shown has a diameter of 0.024", and the thickness of the insulation is 0.047", the diameter over the insulation is
A. 0.107"
B. 0.167"
C. 0.214"
D. 0.238"

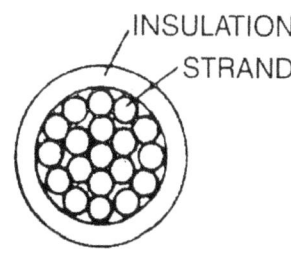

15.____

16. After no. 4, the next larger American Wire Gage size is no.   16._____

    A. 2   B. 3   C. 5   D. 6

17. When steadying a straight wooden ladder for a co-worker who is on it chipping a con-   17._____
    crete wall, it would be LEAST essential for you to wear

    A. rubber gloves   B. hard top shoes
    C. goggles   D. a helmet

18. It would NOT be good practice to use the cutting blade of an electrician's knife to   18._____

    A. cut a template out of cardboard
    B. sharpen a pencil
    C. cut copper wires
    D. remove the braid from an insulated wire

19. You are more likely to receive a shock as the result of a wiring defect in a portable electri-   19._____
    cal device than as the result of a similar defect in a permanently installed device. This is
    so primarily because the

    A. workers on permanent installations are more careful
    B. insulation on portable equipment is usually thinner
    C. metal parts of portable equipment are usually light weight
    D. metal frames of permanent installations are usually grounded

20. If a co-worker is in contact with the 600-volt third rail in the subway, your first action   20._____
    should be to either try to free the man from contact or cut off the power. The action to be
    taken in a particular case will depend primarily on whether

    A. cutting off the power will interfere with train operation
    B. the means of cutting off the power Is nearby
    C. there is any arcing at the point of contact
    D. you can free the man in time to do any good

21. When a number of rubber insulated wires are being pulled into a run of conduit having   21._____
    several sharp bends between the two pull boxes, the pulling is likely to be hard and the
    wires are subjected to considerable strain. For these reasons it is advisable in such a
    case to

    A. push the wires into the feed end of the conduit at the same time that pulling is
       being done
    B. pull in only one wire at a time
    C. use extra heavy grease
    D. pull the wires back a few inches after each forward pull to gain momentum

22. The plug of a portable tool should be removed from the convenience outlet by grasping   22._____
    the plug and not by pulling on the cord because

    A. the plug is easier to grip than the cord
    B. pulling on the cord may allow the plug to fall on the floor and break
    C. pulling on the cord may break the wires off the
    D. plug terminals
    E. the plug is generally better insulated than the cord

23. The best *IMMEDIATE* first aid if electrolyte splashes into the eyes when filling a storage battery is to

    A. bandage the eyes to keep out light
    B. wipe the eyes dry with a soft towel
    C. induce tears to flow by staring at a bright light
    D. bathe the eyes with plenty of clean water

24. Extreme care must be taken when cleaning electrical machine parts indoors with carbon tetrachloride mainly because the fumes

    A. are poisonous
    B. are highly flammable
    C. attack insulation
    D. conduct electricity

25. When using a pipe wrench, the hand should be placed so as to pull instead of push on the wrench. The basis for this recommendation is that there is less likelihood of

    A. the wrench slipping
    B. injury to the hand if the wrench slips
    C. injury to the pipe if the wrench slips
    D. stripped pipe threads

26. In telephoning for assistance because of an accident to a fellow-employee, it is probably most important for you to report the

    A. name of the injured man
    B. time when the accident occurred
    C. cause of the accident
    D. location of the injured man

27. The electrical power for each section of the subway signal system is arranged to come from either one of two supply feeders. The most likely reason for this arrangement is to

    A. divide the load between two power plants
    B. provide continuing service if one feeder goes dead
    C. keep the supply voltage as low as possible
    D. avoid the use of very large cables

28. Present practice with respect to subway lighting switchboards is to make them "dead front." This means that the front of the switchboard has no

    A. metal parts fastened to it
    B. exposed live parts on it
    C. operating handles extending through it
    D. circuit identification markings on it

29. High-voltage switches in power plants are commonly so constructed that their contacts are submerged in oil. The purpose of the oil is to

    A. help quench arcing
    B. lubricate the contacts
    C. cool the switch mechanism
    D. insulate the contacts from the switch framework

30. One type of fire extinguisher used in the subway consists of a steel tank containing compressed carbon dioxide; it has a valve at the top to which is connected a hose and a directing nozzle. The logical way to tell whether such an extinguisher is fully charged is to

    A. tap it lightly
    B. check the inspection tag
    C. weigh it
    D. try it out on a small fire

31. In a storage battery installation consisting of twenty 2-volt cells connected in series, a leak develops in one of the cells and all the electrolyte runs out of it. The terminal voltage across the twenty cells will now be

    A. 40   B. 38   C. 2   D. 0

32. If your foreman gives you an oral order which you do not understand, you should

    A. ask the foreman to put the order in writing
    B. ask the foreman to explain further
    C. ask a fellow employee what he thinks the foreman meant
    D. use your best judgment as that is all that can be expected

33. It is advisable to use a wooden rather than a steel rule when making measurements in the vicinity of electrical machinery. One good reason for this advice is that a wooden rule

    A. will not conduct electricity
    B. can be held in a position by using only one hand
    C. cannot become magnetized
    D. will not damage the machinery if it becomes caught

Items 34 -39.

Items 34 through 39 in Column I are insulating materials each of which is commonly employed for one of the uses listed in Column II. For each insulating material in Column I select its most common use from Column II. *PRINT*, in the correspondingly number item space at the right, the letter given beside your selected use.

Column I (insulating materials)	Column II (uses)
34. Porcelain	A. knive-switch handles
35. Transite	B. commutator-bar separators
36. Wood	C. high voltage line insulators
37. Soft rubber	D. wire and cable insulation
38. Fiber	E. cartridge fuse cases
39. Mica	F. arc chutes

40. If the blade in a hacksaw snaps in two when making a cut, the cause is NOT likely to be that the

    A. teeth were too coarse for work
    B. pressure applied was too great
    C. saw was twisted in the cut
    D. blade was too short for the job

41. When removing the insulation from a wire before making a splice, care should be taken to avoid nicking the wire mainly because then the

    A. current carrying capacity will be reduced
    B. resistance will be increased
    C. insulation will be harder to remove
    D. wire is more likely to break

42. Good practice dictates that an adjustable open end wrench should be used primarily when the

    A. nut to be turned is soft and must not be scored
    B. proper size of fixed wrench is not available
    C. extra leverage is needed
    D. location is cramped permitting only a small turning angle

43. Insulated electrical cables in the subway are sometimes suspended from a tightly strung messenger wire which is supported on brackets attached to the subway structure at intervals of 10 to 20 feet; the electrical cables are strapped to the messenger wire every few inches. By logical reasoning, it is clear that such electrical cables are not suspended overhead without being supported by a messenger wire because the

    A. messenger wire is needed as a continuous ground return
    B. current carrying capacity of unsupported electrical cables would be lower
    C. messenger wire places less strain on the structure
    D. longer spans of electrical cables would sag too much

44. It would generally be poor practice to use ordinary slip-joint pliers to

    A. pull a small nail
    B. bend a wire
    C. remove a cotter pin
    D. tighten a machine bolt

45. The a.c. motor which has exactly the same speed at full-load as at no load is the

    A. synchronous motor
    B. repulsion motor
    C. induction motor
    D. condenser motor

46. A metal bushing is usually screwed on to the end of rigid conduit inside of a junction box. The bushing serves to

    A. center the wires in the conduit
    B. separate the wires where they leave the conduit
    C. protect the wires against abrasion
    D. prevent sagging of the conduit

47. The proper abrasive for cleaning the commutator of a d.c. generator is

    A. steel wool
    B. emery cloth
    C. sand paper
    D. soapstone

48. If a "live" 120-volt d.c. lighting circuit is connected to the 120-volt winding of an otherwise disconnected power transformer, the result will be

   A. blowing of the d.c. circuit fuse
   B. magnetization of the transformer case
   C. sparking at the transformer secondary terminals
   D. burning out of lights on the d.c. circuit

49. Threaded joints in rigid conduit runs are made watertight through the use of

   A. petroleum jelly   B. solder
   C. red lead   D. paraffin wax

50. The most important reason for insisting on neatness in maintenance quarters is that it

   A. decreases the chances of accidents to employees
   B. makes for good employee morale
   C. prevents tools from becoming rusty
   D. increases the available storage space

KEY (CORRECT ANSWERS)

1. D	11. D	21. A	31. D	41. D
2. B	12. B	22. C	32. B	42. B
3. A	13. D	23. D	33. A	43. D
4. C	14. B	24. A	34. C	44. D
5. C	15. C	25. B	35. F	45. A
6. A	16. B	26. D	36. A	46. C
7. D	17. A	27. B	37. D	47. C
8. C	18. C	28. B	38. E	48. A
9. C	19. D	29. A	39. B	49. C
10. D	20. B	30. C	40. D	50. A

MECHANICAL APTITUDE TOOLS AND THEIR USE

EXAMINATION SECTION
TEST 1

Questions 1-16.

DIRECTIONS: Questions 1 through 16 refer to the tools shown below. The numbers in the answers refer to the numbers beneath the tools.
NOTE: These tools are NOT shown to scale

2 (#1)

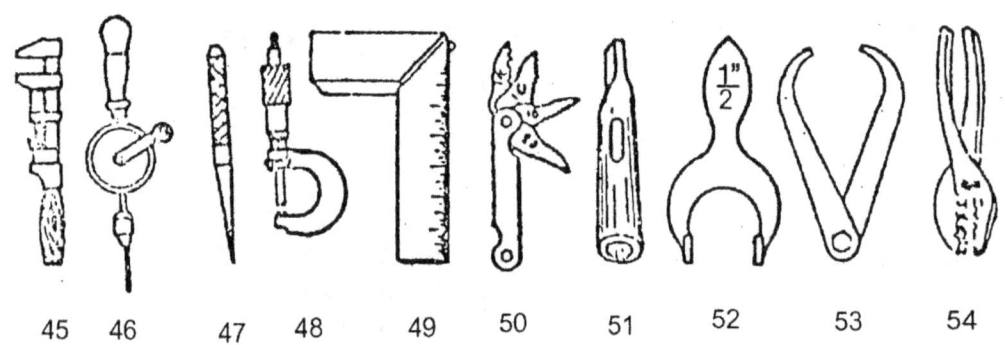

45 46 47 48 49 50 51 52 53 54

1. A 1" x 1" x 1/8" angle iron should be cut by using tool number
   A. 7   B. 12   C. 23   D. 42

2. To peen an iron rivet, you should use tool number
   A. 4   B. 7   C. 21   D. 43

3. The star "drill" is tool number
   A. 5   B. 10   C. 20   D. 22

4. To make holes in sheet metal for sheet metal screws, you should use tool number.
   A. 6   B. 10   C. 36   D. 46

5. To cut through a 3/8" diameter wire rope, you should use tool number
   A. 12   B. 23   C. 42   D. 54

6. To remove cutting burrs from the inside of a steel pipe, you should use tool number
   A. 5   B. 11   C. 14   D. 20

7. The depth of a bored hole may be measured MOST accurately with tool number
   A. 8   B. 16   C. 26   D. 41

8. If the marking on the blade of tool number 7 reads: 12"-32", the 32 refers to the
   A. length   B. thickness   C. weight
   D. number of teeth per inch

9. If tool number 6 bears the mark "5", it should be used to drill holes having a diameter of
   A. 5/32"   B. 5/16"   C. 5/8"   D. 5"

10. To determine MOST quickly the number of threads per inch on a bolt, you should use tool number
    A. 8   B. 16   C. 26   D. 50

11. Wood screws, located in positions where the headroom does not permit the use of an ordinary screwdriver, may be removed by using tool number
    A. 17   B. 28   C. 35   D. 46

12. To remove a broken-off piece of 1/2" diameter pipe from a fitting, you should use tool number

    A. 5   B. 11   C. 20   D. 36

13. The outside diameter of a bushing may be measured MOST accurately with tool number

    A. 8   B. 26   C. 33   D. 43

14. To re-thread a stud hole in the casting of an elevator motor, you should use tool number

    A. 5   B. 20   C. 22   D. 36

15. To enlarge slightly a bored hole in a steel plate, you should use tool number

    A. 5   B. 11   C. 20   D. 36

16. The term "16 oz." should be applied to tool number

    A. 1   B. 12   C. 21   D. 42

KEYS (CORRECT ANSWERS)

1.	A	9.	B
2.	C	10.	D
3.	B	11.	C
4.	D	12.	C
5.	B	13.	C
6.	B	14.	D
7.	B	15.	A
8.	D	16.	C

TEST 2

Questions 1-11.

DIRECTIONS: Questions 1 through 11 refer to the instruments listed below. Each instrument is listed with an identifying number in front of it.

  1 - Hygrometer
  2 - Ammeter
  3 - Voltmeter
  4 - Wattmeter
  5 - Megger
  6 - Oscilloscope
  7 - Frequency meter
  8 - Micrometer
  9 - Vernier calliper
  10 - Wire gage
  11 - 6-foot folding rule
  12 - Architect's scale
  13 - Planimeter
  14 - Engineer's scale
  15 - Ohmmeter

1. The instrument that should be used to *accurately* measure the resistance of a 4,700-ohm resistor is number
   A. 3 B. 4 C. 7 D. 15

2. To measure the current in an electrical circuit, the instrument that should be used is number
   A. 2 B. 7 C. 8 D. 15

3. To measure the insulation resistance of a rubber-covered electrical cable, the instrument that should be used is number
   A. 4 B. 5 C. 8 D. 15

4. An AC motor is hooked up to a power distribution box. In order to check the voltage at the motor terminals, the instrument that should be used is number
   A. 2 B. 3 C. 4 D. 7

5. To measure the shaft diameter of a motor *accurately* to one-thousandth of an inch, the instrument that should be used is number
   A. 8 B. 10 C. 11 D. 14

6. The instrument that should be used to determine whether 25 Hz. or 60 Hz. is present in an electrical circuit is number
   A. 4 B. 5 C. 7 D. 8

7. Of the following, the *proper* instrument to use to determine the diameter of the conductor of a piece of electrical hookup wire is number
   A. 10 B. 11 C. 12 D. 14

8. The amount of electrical power being used in a balanced three-phase circuit should be measured with number
   A. 2 B. 3 C. 4 D. 5

9. The electrical wave form at a given point in an electronic circuit can be observed with number
   A. 2 B. 3 C. 6 D. 7

10. The *proper* instrument to use for measuring the width of a door is number   10.____

    A. 11   B. 12   C. 13   D. 14

11. A one-inch hole with a tolerance of plus or minus three-thousandths is reamed in a steel   11.____
    block. The *proper* instrument to accurately check the diameter of the hole is number

    A. 8   B. 9   C. 11   D. 14

12. An oilstone is LEAST likely to be used correctly to sharpen a   12.____

    A. scraper   B. chisel   C. knife   D. saw

13. To cut the ends of a number of lengths of wood at an angle of 45 degrees, it would be   13.____
    BEST to use a

    A. mitre-box   B. protractor C. triangle   D. wooden rule

14. A gouge is a tool used for   14.____

    A. planing wood smooth   B. grinding metal
    C. drilling steel   D. chiseling wood

15. Holes are usually countersunk when installing   15.____

    A. carriage bolts   B. lag screws
    C. flat-head screws   D. square nuts

16. A tool that is *generally* used to slightly elongate a round hole in scrap-iron is a   16.____

    A. rat-tail file   B. reamer   C. drill   D. rasp

17. When the term "10-24" is used to specify a machine screw, the number 24 refers to the   17.____

    A. number of screws per pound B. diameter of the screw
    C. length of the screw   D. number of threads per inch

18. If you were unable to tighten a nut by means of a ratchet wrench because, although the   18.____
    nut turned on with the forward movement of the wrench, it turned off with the backward
    movement, you should

    A. make the nut hand-tight before using the wrench
    B. reverse the ratchet action
    C. put a few drops of oil on the wrench
    D. use a different socket in the handle

19. If you were installing a long wood screw and found you were unable to drive this screw   19.____
    more than three-quarters of its length by the use of a properly-fitting straight-handled
    screwdriver, the *proper* SUBSEQUENT action would be for you to

    A. take out the screw and put soap on it
    B. change to the use of a screwdriver-bit and brace
    C. take out the screw and drill a shorter hole before redriving
    D. use a pair of pliers on the blade of the screwdriver

20. Good practice requres that the end of a pipe to be installed in a plumbing system be reamed to remove the inside burr after it has been cut to length. The *purpose* of this reaming is to

    A. restore the original inside diameter of the pipe at the end
    B. remove loose rust
    C. make the threading of the pipe easier
    D. finish the pipe accurately to length

20.____

KEYS (CORRECT ANSWERS)

1.	D	11.	B
2.	A	12.	D
3.	B	13.	A
4.	B	14.	D
5.	A	15.	C
6.	C	16.	A
7.	A	17.	D
8.	C	18.	A
9.	C	19.	A
10.	A	20.	A

ARITHMETICAL REASONING

EXAMINATION SECTION
TEST 1

DIRECTIONS: Each question or incomplete statement is followed by several suggested answers or completions. Select the one that BEST answers the question or completes the statement. *PRINT THE LETTER OF THE CORRECT ANSWER IN THE SPACE AT THE RIGHT.*

1. A canvas tarpaulin measures 6 feet by 9 feet.
   The LARGEST circular area that can be covered completely by this tarpaulin is a circle with a diameter of _____ feet.

   A. 9   B. 8   C. 7   D. 6

   1.____

2. The population of Maple Grove was 1,000 in 2006. In 2007, the population increased 40 percent, but in 2008, 2009, and 2010, the population decreased 20 percent, 10 percent, and 25 percent, respectively. (For each year, the percentage change in population is based upon a comparison with the preceding year.)
   At the end of this period, the population was MOST NEARLY

   A. 900   B. 850   C. 800   D. 750

   2.____

3. The ratio of boys to girls in one school is 6 to 4. A second school contains half as many boys and twice as many girls as the first.
   The one of the following statements that is MOST accurate is that

   A. both schools have the same number of pupils
   B. the first school has 10 percent more pupils than the second
   C. the second school has 10 percent more pupils than the first
   D. there is not sufficient information to reach any conclusion about which school has more pupils

   3.____

4. In a certain city, X number of cases of malaria have occurred over a 10-year period, resulting in Y number of deaths.
   The AVERAGE annual death rate from malaria in this city is

   A. Y/10   B. 10/X   C. 10-X/Y   D. $\frac{Y(10X)}{X+Y}$

   4.____

5. A firemen's softball team wins 6 games out of the first 9 played. They go on to win all their remaining games and finish the season with a final average of games won of .750.
   The TOTAL number of games they played that season was

   A. 10   B. 12   C. 15   D. 18

   5.____

6. While inspecting a cylindrical gravity tank for an automatic sprinkler system, a chief observes that the water in the tank is 10 feet deep and that the tank has a diameter of 9 feet. He asks the building manager how many gallons are in the tank and receives the reply, *About 10,000.* (Cubic foot of water contains 7 1/2 gallons.) Based on his own observation and calculations, the chief should

   6.____

A. agree that the manager's answer is probably correct
B. disagree with the manager's answer; the answer is more nearly 20,000 gallons
C. disagree with the manager's answer; the answer is more nearly 15,000 gallons
D. disagree with the manager's answer; the answer is more nearly 5,000 gallons

7. The diagram at the right represents the storage space of a fire engine. The amount of space available for the storage of hose in the fire engine is MOST NEARLY _____ cubic feet.
   A. 40
   B. 75
   C. 540
   D. 600

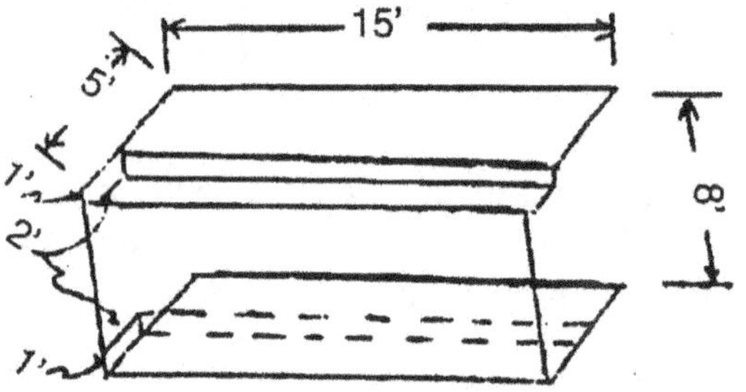

8. If a piece of rope 100 feet long is cut so that one piece is 2/3 as long as the other piece, the length of the longer piece must be _____ feet.

   A. 60   B. 66 2/3   C. 70   D. 75

9. A water tank has a discharge valve which is capable of emptying the tank when full in two hours. It also has an inlet valve which can fill the tank, when empty, in four hours and a second inlet valve which can fill the tank, when empty, in six hours.
   If the tank is full and all three valves are opened fully, with water flowing through each valve to capacity, the tank will be emptied in _____ hours.

   A. 2
   B. 6
   C. 12
   D. a period of time which cannot be determined from the information given

10. Final grades in a history course are determined as follows:
    Class recitations - weight 50
    Weekly quizzes - weight 25
    Final examination - weight 25
    A student has an average of 60 on a class recitation and 80 on weekly quizzes.
    In order to receive a final grade of 75, he must obtain on his final examination a grade of

    A. 75   B. 80   C. 90   D. 100

11. Suppose that 8 inches of snow contribute as much water to the reservoir system as one inch of rain.
    If, during a snowstorm, an average of 12 inches of snow fell during a six-hour period, with drifts as high as three feet, the addition to the water supply as a result of this snowfall ultimately will be the equivalent of _____ inches of rain.

    A. 1 1/2
    B. 3
    C. 4 1/2
    D. an amount of rain which cannot be determined from the information given

12. A fire engine carries 900 feet of 2 1/2" hose, 500 feet of 2" hose, and 350 feet of 1 1/2" hose.
    Of the total hose carried, the percentage of 1 1/2" hose is MOST NEARLY

    A. 35   B. 30   C. 25   D. 20

    12.____

13. An engine company made 96 runs in the month of April, which was a decrease of 20% from the number of runs made in March.
    The number of runs made in March was MOST NEARLY

    A. 136   B. 128   C. 120   D. 110

    13.____

14. A water tank has a capacity of 6,000 gallons. Connected to the tank is a pump capable of supplying water at the rate of 25 gallons per minute, which goes into operation automatically when the water in the tank falls to the one-half mark.
    If we start with a full tank and drain the water from the tank at the rate of 50 gallons a minute, the tank can continue supplying water at the required rate for _____ hours.

    A. 2 1/2   B. 3   C. 3 1/2   D. 4

    14.____

15. Three firemen are assigned the task of cleaning fire apparatus which usually takes three men five hours to complete. After they have been working three hours, three additional firemen are assigned to help them. Assuming that they all work at the normal rate, the assignment of the additional men will reduce the time required to complete the task by _____ minutes.

    A. 20   B. 30   C. 50   D. 60

    15.____

16. Assume that at the beginning of the calendar year, an employee was earning $48,000 per year. On July 1st, he received an increase of $2,400 per year. On November 1st, he was promoted to a position paying $60,000 per year. The total earnings for the year were MOST NEARLY

    A. $51,000   B. $49,000   C. $50,000   D. $53,000

    16.____

17. Engine A leaves its firehouse at 1:48 P.M. and travels 3 miles to a fire at an average speed of 30 miles per hour. Engine B leaves its firehouse at 1:51 P.M. and travels 6 miles to the same fire at an average speed of 40 miles per hour.
    From the above facts, we may conclude that Engine A arrives _____ minutes _____ Engine B.

    A. 3; before
    B. 6; before
    C. 3; after
    D. 6; after

    17.____

18. A widely used formula for calculating the quantity of water discharged from a hose is
    GPM = $29.7d^2 / P$, where GPM = gallons per minute, d = diameter of the nozzle in inches, and P = pressure at the nozzle in pounds per square inch.
    If it takes 1 minute to extinguish a fire using a 1 1/2" nozzle at 100 pounds pressure per square inch, the number of gallons discharged is, according to the above formula, MOST NEARLY

    A. 730   B. 650   C. 690   D. 670

    18.____

19. The spring of a spring balance will stretch in proportion to the amount of weight placed on the balance.
    If a 2-pound weight placed on a certain balance stretches the spring 1/4", then a stretch in the spring of 1 3/4" will be caused by a weight of _____ lbs.

    A. 10   B. 12   C. 14   D. 16

20. In a yard 100 feet by 60 feet, a dog is tied by a leash to a stake driven into the ground in the center of the yard.
    If the dog is to be kept from going off the property, the MAXIMUM acceptable length of the leash is _____ feet.

    A. 60   B. 50   C. 30   D. 28

21. From a length of pipe 10 feet long, a 3 1/3 foot piece is to be cut.
    If the diameter of the 10-foot length is 5 inches, the diameter of the piece to be cut will be

    A. 5"   B. 2 1/3"   C. 2"   D. 1 2/3"

22. A certain crew consists of one foreman who is paid $15.00 per hour, 2 carpenters who are paid $12.60 per hour, 4 helpers who are paid $10.50 per hour, and 10 laborers who are paid $7.50 per hour.
    The average hourly earnings of the members of the crew is MOST NEARLY

    A. $11.40   B. $10.50   C. $10.05   D. $9.30

23. The fraction which is equivalent to the sum of .125, .25, .375, and .0625 is

    A. 5/8   B. 13/16   C. 7/8   D. 15/16

24. If the pay period of an employee is changed from every two weeks to twice a month, his gross pay (before deductions) from each pay period will

    A. increase by one-tenth
    B. increase by one-twelfth
    C. decrease by one-thirteenth
    D. decrease by one-fifteenth

25. In a certain state, the automobile license tags consist of two letters followed by three digits, e.g., AA-122. The MAXIMUM number of different combinations of numbers and letters which can be obtained under this system is MOST NEARLY

    A. 13,500   B. 75,000   C. 325,000   D. 675,000

KEY (CORRECT ANSWERS)

1. D
2. D
3. C
4. A
5. B

6. D
7. C
8. A
9. C
10. D

11. A
12. D
13. C
14. B
15. D

16. A
17. B
18. D
19. C
20. C

21. A
22. D
23. B
24. B
25. D

SOLUTIONS TO PROBLEMS

1. The largest circular area completely covered by the tarpaulin would have a diameter of the lesser of 6 ft. and 9 ft.

2. At the end of 2010, the population was $(1000)(1.40)(.80)(.90)(.75) = 756 \approx 750$.

3. Let 6x and 4x represent the number of boys and girls, respectively, at the first school. Then, 3x and 8x will represent the number of boys and girls, respectively, at the second school. The enrollment of the second school, 11x, is 10% higher than the enrollment at the first school, 10x.

4. Since Y deaths have occurred over a 10-year period due to malaria, the annual death rate caused by malaria is Y/10. X, the number of cases of malaria, has no effect on the annual death rate.

5. Let x = number of games played, after the first 9 games. Then, $(6+x)/(9+x) = .750$. Solving, x = 3. The total number of games played = 9 + 3 = 12.

6. Volume = $(\pi)(4.5)^2(10) \approx 636$ cu.ft. Then, $(636)(7\ 1/2) = 4770 \approx 5000$

7. 15x8x3 = 360; 15x6x2 = 180; 360 + 180 = 540 cu.ft.

8. Let 2x and 3x represent the two pieces. Then, 2x + 3x = 100. Solving, x = 20. The longer piece = (3)(20) = 60 ft.

9. Let x = number of hours required. Then, $\frac{x}{2} \cdot \frac{x}{4} \cdot \frac{x}{6} = 1$ Simplifying, x/12 = 1. Thus, x = 12

10. Let x = final exam grade. Then, (60)(.50) + (80)(.25) + (x)(.25) = 75. Simplifying, 50 + ,25x = 75. Solving, x = 100

11. If 8 in. of snow contribute 1 in. of rain, then 12 in. of snow contribute (1)(12/8) = 1 1/2 in. of rain.

12. 350 ÷ (900+500+350) = .20 = 20%

13. The number of runs in March was 96 ÷ .80 = 120

14. The time required to extract 3000 gallons at 50 gallons per minute = 3000 ÷ 50 = 60 min. = 1 hour. At this point, the tank is half full. Also, a pump begins replenishing the tank at 25 gallons per minute. Thus, the effect on draining has been slowed to 50 - 25 = 25 gallons per minute. To drain the remaining 3000 gallons will require 3000 ÷ 25 = 120 minutes = 2 hours. Total draining time = 3 hours.

15. (3)(5) = 15 man-hours. After 3 hours, 9 man-hours have been used. At this point, 6 men are working, and since only 6 man-hours remaining, the time needed is 1 hour = 60 minutes.

7 (#1)

16. ($48,000)(1/2) + ($50,400)(1/3) + ($60,000)(1/6) = $50,800 ≈ $51,000

17. Engine A requires (3)(60/30) = 6 minutes to get to the fire.
So, Engine A arrives at 1:54 PM. Engine B requires (6)(60/40) = 9 minutes to get to the fire. So, Engine B arrives at 2:00 PM. Thus, Engine A arrives 6 minutes before Engine B.

18. GPM = $(29.7)(1.5)^2(\sqrt{100})$ = 668.25 ≈ 670

19. Let x = required number of pounds. Then, 2/x = 1/4/1 3/4.
So, 1/4x = 3 1/2. Solving, x = 14

20. The shorter of the two dimensions is 60 ft. If the dog is in the center of the yard, the maximum length allowed for the leash is 60/2 = 30 ft.

21. The diameter of the cut piece = diameter of entire pipe = 5"

22. [($15.00)(1)+($12.60)(2)+($10.50)(4)+($7.50)(10)]/17 = $157.20/17 9.25 (closest answer in answer key is $9.30).

23. .125 + .25 + .375 + .0625 = .8125 = 13/16

24. Let x = annual pay. Then, x/26 = pay every two weeks, whereas pay every half month. His increase is $\frac{x}{24} - \frac{x}{26} = \frac{x}{312}$, which represents a fractional increase of $\frac{x}{312} / \frac{x}{26} = \frac{1}{12}$

25. The number of different license tags = (26)(26)(10)(10)(10) = 676,000 (closest answer in answer key is 675,000).

TEST 2

DIRECTIONS: Each question or incomplete statement is followed by several suggested answers or completions. Select the one that BEST answers the question or completes the statement. *PRINT THE LETTER OF THE CORRECT ANSWER IN THE SPACE AT THE RIGHT.*

1. If cast iron weighs 450 pounds per cubic foot, the weight of a solid cast iron manhole cover 2 feet in diameter and 1 inch thick is MOST NEARLY _____ pounds.

    A. 94   B. 118   C. 136   D. 164

2. The sum of 2 5/8, 3 3/16, 1 1/2, and 4 1/4 is

    A. 9 13/16   B. 10 7/16   C. 11 9/16   D. 13 3/16

3. A pump is able to fill a tank holding 15,000 gallons in 2 hours and 30 minutes. Pumping at the same rate, an empty 60,000 gallon tank can be filled in

    A. 10 hours
    B. 10 hours, 30 minutes
    C. 11 hours
    D. 11 hours, 30 minutes

4. Assume you want to add 10,000 gallons of water to a tank. If you pump water into the tank at the rate of 100 gallons per minute for one hour and 50 gallons per minute after the first hour, the total time required to add the 10,000 gallons is MOST NEARLY

    A. 1 hour, 20 minutes
    B. 2 hours
    C. 2 hours, 20 minutes
    D. 3 hours

5. A tank 25 feet long, 15 feet wide, and 10 feet deep is enlarged by extending the length another 25 feet.
    The enlarged tank will be able to hold _____ more than the original tank.

    A. 50%   B. 100%   C. 150%   D. 200%

6. If cast iron weighs 450 pounds per cubic foot, the weight of a solid cast iron manhole cover 4 feet in diameter and 1 inch thick is MOST NEARLY _____ pounds.

    A. 188   B. 236   C. 328   D. 471

7. If four men work seven hours during the day, the number of man-hours of work done is

    A. 4   B. 7   C. 11   D. 28

8. If it takes four men fourteen days to do a certain job, seven men working at the same rate should be able to do the same job in _____ days.

    A. 8   B. 7   C. 6   D. 5

9. A truck leaves the garage at 9:26 A.M. and returns the same day at 3:43 P.M. The period of time that the truck was away from the garage is MOST NEARLY _____ hours, _____ minutes.

    A. 5; 17   B. 5; 43   C. 6; 17   D. 6; 26

10. Assume that it takes 6 men 8 days to do a certain job. Working at the same speed, the number of days that it will take 4 men to do this job is

    A. 9   B. 10   C. 12   D. 14

11. The sum of 3 5/8 + 4 1/4 + 6 1/2 + 7 1/8 is

    A. 20 7/8   B. 21 1/4   C. 21 1/2   D. 22 1/8

12. The fraction which is equal to .0625 is

    A. 1/64   B. 3/64   C. 1/16   D. 5/8

13. The volume, in cubic feet, of a rectangular coal bin 8 feet long by 5 feet wide by 7 feet high is MOST NEARLY

    A. 40   B. 56   C. 186   D. 280

14. Assume that a car travels at a constant speed of 36 miles per hour.
    The speed of this car, in feet per second, is MOST NEARLY (one mile equals 5,280 ft.)

    A. 3   B. 24.6   C. 52.8   D. 879.8

15. If one-third of a 19-foot length of lumber is cut off, the length of the remaining piece will measure APPROXIMATELY

    A. 8'8"   B. 9'8"   C. 12'8"   D. 13'8"

16. The circumference of a circle having a diameter of 10" is MOST NEARLY _____ inches.

    A. 3.14   B. 18.72   C. 24.96   D. 31.4

17. Assume that in the purchase of paint, the seller quotes a discount of 10%.
    If the price per gallon is $19.05, the actual payment, in dollars per gallon, is MOST NEARLY

    A. $17.15   B. $17.85   C. $18.75   D. $19.50

18. Assume that a cubic foot of water contains 7 1/2 gallons. The number of gallons of water which could be contained in a rectangular tank 3 feet long, 2 feet wide, and 2 feet deep is MOST NEARLY

    A. 12   B. 45   C. 90   D. 120

19. The volume, in cubic feet, of a slab of concrete that is 5'0" wide, 6'0" long, and 0'6" in depth is MOST NEARLY

    A. 15.0   B. 13.5   C. 12.0   D. 10.5

20. The sum of the following pipe lengths, 22 1/8", 7 3/4", 19 7/16", and 43 5/8", is

    A. 91 7/8"   B. 92 1/16"   C. 92 1/2"   D. 92 15/16"

21. The area, in square feet, of a plant floor that is 42 feet wide and 75 feet long is

    A. 3,150   B. 3,100   C. 3.075   D. 2,760

22. The sum of the following dimensions, 1 5/8, 2 1/4, 4 1/16, and 3 3/16, is

    A. 10 15/16   B. 11   C. 11 1/8   D. 11 1/4

23. Assume that six men, working together at the same rate of speed, can complete a certain job in 3 hours.
If, however, there were only four men available to do this job, and they all worked at the same rate of speed, to complete this job would take MOST NEARLY _____ hours.

   A. 4 1/4   B. 4 1/2   C. 4 3/4   D. 5

24. Due to unforeseen difficulties, a job which would normally take 17 hours to complete was actually completed in 21 hours.
This represents a percent increase over the normal time of MOST NEARLY

   A. 19%   B. 2.4%   C. 24%   D. 124%

25. Truck A costs $30,000 and gets 12 mpg and truck B costs $35,000 and gets 15 mpg. After 1 year driving 12,000 miles, how much would be saved by purchasing truck A if gasoline costs $1.50 per gallon?

   A. $1,000   B. $3,000   C. $4,700   D. $6,000

KEY (CORRECT ANSWERS)

1. B
2. C
3. A
4. C
5. B

6. D
7. D
8. A
9. C
10. C

11. C
12. C
13. D
14. C
15. C

16. D
17. A
18. C
19. A
20. D

21. A
22. C
23. B
24. C
25. C

SOLUTIONS TO PROBLEMS

1. $(450)(\pi)(1)^2(1/12) \approx 118$ pounds. (Note: $V = \pi R^2 H$)

2. 2 5/8 + 3 3/16 + 1 1/2 + 4 1/4 = 10 25/16 = 11 9/16

3. To fill a 60,000 gallon tank would require (4)(2 1/2 hrs.) = 10 hrs.

4. After 1 hour, (100)(60) = 6000 gallons have been added. To add the remaining 4000 gallons will require 4000 ÷ 50 = 80 minutes = 1 hour 20 minutes. Thus, total time needed is 2 hrs. 20 min.

5. The original volume = (25)(15)(10) = 3750 cu.ft., and the new volume = (50)(15)(10) = 7500 cu.ft. The increased volume of 3750 represents an increase of (3750/3750)(100) = 100%.

6. $(450)(\pi)(2)^2(1/12) \approx 471$ pounds

7. (4)(7) = 28 man-hours

8. (4)(14) = 56 man-days. Then, 56 ÷ 7 = 8 days

9. From 9:26 A.M. to 3:43 P.M. = 6 hrs. 17 min.

10. (6)(8) = 48 man-days. Then, 48 ÷ 4 = 12 days

11. 3 5/8 + 4 1/4 + 6 1/2 + 7 1/8 = 20 12/8 = 21 1/2

12. .0625 = 625/10,000 = 1/16

13. (8)(5)(7) = 280 cu.ft.

14. (36)(5280) = 190,080 ft. per hour. Since there are 3600 seconds in 1 hour, the speed = 190,080 ÷ 3600 = 52.8 ft. per second.

15. 19' - 1/3(19') = 12 2/3, = 12'8"

16. Circumference = $(\pi)(10")$ 31.4"

17. ($19.05)(.90) ≈ $17.15

18. (7 1/2)(3)(2)(2) = 90 gallons

19. (5)(6)(1/2) = 15 cu.ft.

20. 22 1/8" + 7 3/4" + 19 7/16" + 43 5/8" = 91 31/16" = 92 15/16"

21. Area = (42)(75) = 3150 sq.ft.

5 (#2)

22. 1 5/8 + 2 1/4 + 4 1/16 + 3 3/16 = 10 18/16 = 11 1/8

23. (6) (3) = 18 man-hours. Then, 18 / 4 = 4 1/2 hours

24. 21 - 17 = 4. Then, 4/17 ≈ 24%

25. For Truck A, the expenses are $30,000 + (1000)($1.50) = $31,500 For Truck B, the expenses are $35,000 + (800)($1.50) = $36,200. $36,200 - $31,500 = $4,700

TEST 3

DIRECTIONS: Each question or incomplete statement is followed by several suggested answers or completions. Select the one that BEST answers the question or completes the statement. *PRINT THE LETTER OF THE CORRECT ANSWER IN THE SPACE AT THE RIGHT.*

1. Assume that a light maintainer and his helper replaced 25 lamps on one round of their assigned territory.
   If it took two hours to complete this round, and the maintainer's pay rate was $9.60 per hour and the helper's rate was $8.40 per hour, the labor cost of replacing each burned out lamp averaged _____ cents.

   A. 18   B. 36   C. 72   D. 144

2. A certain power distribution job will require two main-tainers at $16.00 per hour and two helpers at $13.20 per hour. The job will take three 8-hour days to complete and will require 6 hours of planning and supervision by a foreman at $19.60 per hour.
   The TOTAL labor cost for this job is

   A. $264.80   B. $501.60   C. $818.40   D. $1,519.20

3. Two identical containers are partly filled with bolts and weigh 40 lbs. and 75 lbs., respectively. To save storage space, all the bolts are put in one of the containers. The two containers now weigh 5 lbs. and 110 lbs., respectively.
   If three bolts weigh 1/2 lb., the TOTAL number of bolts is

   A. 210   B. 450   C. 630   D. 660

4. The sum of the following dimensions, 2'7 1/2", 1'8 1/2", 2'1/16", and 3/4", is

   A. 5'15 9/16"   B. 5'15 11/16"
   C. 5'7/16"   D. 6'4 9/16"

5. If a 3-foot length of contact rail weighs 150 pounds, then 39 feet of contact rail weighs _____ pounds.

   A. 1,850   B. 1,900   C. 1,950   D. 2,000

6. The sum of the following dimensions, 3'2 1/2", 8 7/8", 2'6 3/8", 2'9 3/4", and 1'0", is

   A. 9'3 1/4"   B. 10'3 1/4"   C. 10'7 1/4"   D. 16'7 1/4"

7. If a drawing for a contact rail installation is made to a scale of 1 1/2" to the foot, the drawing is said to be one _____ size.

   A. sixteenth   B. eight   C. quarter   D. half

8. If a drawing has a scale of 1/4" = 1', a dimension of 1 3/4" on the drawing would be equal to

   A. 4'   B. 5'   C. 6'   D. 7'

9. A reel weighs 600 lbs. when fully loaded with cable and 200 lbs. when empty.
   If the cable weighs 2.5 lbs. per foot, the number of reels a foreman should order for a job requiring 700 feet of this cable is _____ reels.

   A. 2   B. 3   C. 4   D. 5

10. If the scale on a working drawing is shown as 1/4" = 1', a scaled measurement of 4 1/2 inches represents an actual length of _____ feet.

    A. 8   B. 9   C. 16   D. 18

11. A gap on the third rail starts at a subway column marked 217+79. The gap extends 68 feet to another column marked 217+11.
    A column midway between these columns would be marked 217+_____

    A. 34   B. 39   C. 45   D. 68

12. Assume a foreman decided that 100 contact rail ties need replacing. Each tie measures 9' x 6" x 8".
    In providing room for storing these ties at the job site, the MINIMUM storage volume required is APPROXIMATELY _____ cubic feet.

    A. 300   B. 360   C. 432   D. 576

13. Assume a certain job was done a year ago and took 8 men a total of 5 days to complete. The records show that each day involved 5 hours of overtime for half the men. Your assistant supervisor now assigns you the identical job to be done using 6 men and no overtime.
    The MINIMUM number of regular work days that should be scheduled for this job is _____ days.

    A. 13   B. 11   C. 9   D. 6

14. The sum of the following dimensions, 12'11 3/16", 9'8 5/8", 7'3 3/4", 5'2 1/2", and 3'1 1/4", is

    A. 39'5 9/16"   B. 38'3 5/16"
    C. 36'2 3/8"   D. 35'1 7/8"

15. If the scale on a drawing is 1/4" to the foot, then a 5/8" measurement would represent an actual length of

    A. 5'4"   B. 4'8"   C. 2'6"   D. 1'3"

16. The sum of 1 9/16", 3 1/2", 7 3/8", 10 3/4", and 12 5/8" is

    A. 33 11/16"   B. 34 13/16"   C. 35 11/16"   D. 35 13/16"

17. A reel containing an unknown length of cable weighs 340 pounds.
    If the empty reel weighs 119 lbs. and the cable weighs 0.85 lb. per foot, the number of feet of cable on the reel is

    A. 140   B. 260   C. 400   D. 540

18. If the scale on a shop drawing is 1/4" to the foot, then a part which measures 3 3/8 inches long on the drawing has an actual length of_____ feet _____ inches.

    A. 12; 6   B. 13; 6   C. 13; 9   D. 14; 9

19. Taking into account time and one-half payment for time over 40 hours of work, the gross pay of an employee who works 43 hours in a week at a rate of pay of $5.34 per hour is

    A. $213.60   B. $229.62   C. $237.63   D. $245.64

20. The sum of 0.365 + 3.941 + 10.676 + 0.784 is

    A. 13.766   B. 15.666   C. 15.756   D. 15.766

    20.____

21. An air conditioning unit is rated at 1000 watts. The unit is run for 10 hours per day, five days per week. If the cost for electrical energy is 50 cents per kilowatt-hour, the weekly cost for electricity should be

    A. $2.50   B. $5.00   C. $25.00   D. $250.00

    21.____

22. Assume that the cost of a certain wiring installation is broken down as follows: Materials $1,200, Labor $800, and Rental of equipment $400.
    The percentage of the total cost of the job that can be charged to Labor is MOST NEARLY

    A. 12.3   B. 33.3   C. 40.0   D. 66.6

    22.____

23. Assume that it takes 4 electrician's helpers 6 days to do a certain job.
    Working at the same rate of speed, the number of days it will take 3 electrician's helpers to do the same job is

    A. 6   B. 7   C. 8   D. 9

    23.____

24. Assume that a 120-volt, 25-cycle magnetic coil is to be rewound to operate properly on 60-cycles at the same voltage.
    If the coil at 25-cycles has 1,000 turns, at 60-cycles the number of turns should be MOST NEARLY

    A. 2,400   B. 1,200   C. 416   D. 208

    24.____

25. A light maintainer whose rate is $14.40 per hour is assigned to replace burned-out station and tunnel lamps. During 4 hours, he replaces 28 lamps.
    The average labor cost for replacing each of these burned-out lamps was NEAREST to

    A. 56¢   B. $1.04   C. $2.00   D. $3.60

    25.____

KEY (CORRECT ANSWERS)

1. D
2. D
3. C
4. D
5. C

6. B
7. B
8. D
9. D
10. D

11. C
12. A
13. C
14. B
15. C

16. D
17. B
18. B
19. C
20. D

21. C
22. B
23. C
24. C
25. C

SOLUTIONS TO PROBLEMS

1. (2)($9.60+$8.40) = $36.00. Then, $36.00 ÷ 25 = $1.44 or 144 cents.

2. (2)($16.00)(24) + (2)($13.20)(24) + (6)($19.60) = $1519.20

3. An empty container weighs 5 lbs., so the container which contains bolts and weighs 110 lbs. actually has 105 lbs. of bolts. Since 3 bolts weigh 1/2 lb., 105 lbs. would contain (105/1/2)(3) = 630 bolts.

4. 2'7 1/4" + 1'8 1/2" + 2'1/16" + 3/4" = 5'15 25/16" = 6 '4 9/16"

5. 39 feet of rail weighs (13)(150) = 1950 pounds

6. 3'2 1/4" + 8 7/8" + 2'6 3/8" + 2'9 3/4" + 1'0" = 8'25 18/8" = 10'3 1/4"

7. 1 1/2"/1" = 3/2.1/12=1/8

8. 1 3/4" ÷ 1/4" = 7 Then, (7)(1') = 7'

9. 600 - 200 = 400. Then, 400 ÷ 2.5 = 160 ft. of cable per reel. Since 700 ft. of cable is needed, 700/160 = 4.375, which means 5 reels will be required (must round up).

10. 4 1/2" ÷ 1/4" = 9/2 4/1 = 18 Then, (18)(1') = 18'

11. Half of 68 = 34; 11 + 34 = 45; 79 - 34 = 45

12. (100)(9')(1/2')(2/3') = 300 cu.ft.

13. Number of man-days = (4)(5) + (4)(5)(1 5/8) =52.5
    For 6 men working only 8-hour days, 52.5 ÷ 6 = 8.75 = 9 days needed.

14. 12'11 3/16" + 9'8 5/8" + 7'3 3/4" + 5'2 1/2" + 3'1 1/4" = 36'25 37/16" = 38'3 5/16"

15. 5/8" ÷ 1/4" = 5/8 . 4/1 = 2 1/2. Then, (2 1/2)(1') = 2'6"

16. 1 9/16" + 3 1/2" + 7 3/8" + 10 3/4" + 12 5/8" = 33 45/16" = 35 13/36"

17. 340 - 119 = 221 lbs. Then, 221 ÷ .85 = 260 ft.

18. 3 3/8" ÷ 1/4" = 27/8 . 4/1 = 13/ 1/2. Then, (13 1/2) (1') = 13 ft. 6 in.

19. (40)($5.34) + (3)($5.34)(1.5) = $237.63

20. 0.365 +3.941 + 10.676 + 0.784 = 15.766

21. (1000)(10)(5) = 50,000 watt-hours = 50 kilowatt-hours. Then, (50)($.50) = $25.00

22. $800 / ($1200+$800+$400) =1/3 ≈ 33.3%

23. (4)(6) = 24. Then, 24/ 3 = 8 days

24. Let x = number of required turns. Since the number of cycles varies inversely as the number of turns, 25/60 = x/1000.
Solving, x 416 (actually 416 2/3)

25. ($14.40)(4) = $57.60. Then, $57.60 ÷ 28 ≈ $2.06

ELECTRO-MECHANICAL NOTES AND RESOURCES

TABLE OF CONTENTS

		Page
I.	**BASIC ELECTRICITY**	1
	Ohm's Law	2
	Kirchoff's Voltage Law	3
	Kirchoff's Current Law	3
	Inductors	3
	Capacitors	4
	AC Cycles	4
	Magnetism	5
	Relays	6
	Switches	6
	Diodes	6
	Transistors	7
	Soldering	8
II.	**COMPUTERS**	8
	Numbering Systems	9
	Flip Flops	10
	Logic Gates	12
III.	**OSCILLOSCOPES**	12
	Meters	13
IV.	**SCIENTIFIC NOTATION**	14
V.	**GEARS**	14
	Pulleys	16
	Lubricants	18

ELECTRO-MECHANICAL NOTES AND RESOURCES
I. BASIC ELECTRICITY

Resistance is measured in ohms, and its symbol is Ω. Resistance is additive in series circuits. This means that with two resistors in series as shown below, if one resistor is 100Ω's and the other 200Ω's, then the total resistance is 300Ω's.

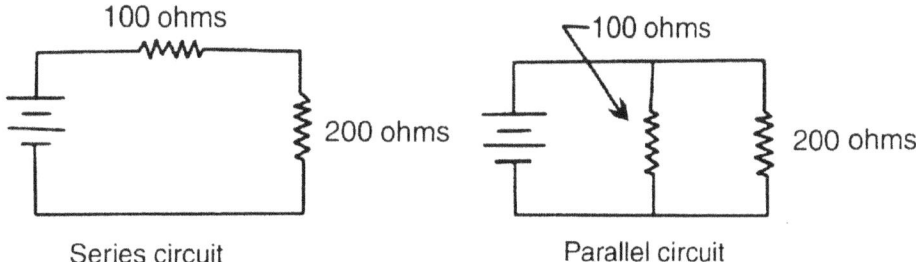

Series circuit   Parallel circuit

Resistance in parallel is summed differently. In the figure shown above in the parallel circuit, if the 100 ohm resistor is considered to be R, and the 200 ohm resistor is R, the formula is:

$$\frac{1}{R_t} = \frac{1}{R_1} + \frac{1}{R_2}.$$

Derivation is as follows:

$$\frac{1}{R_1} = (\frac{1}{R_1} \times \frac{R_2}{R_2}) + (\frac{1}{R_2} \times \frac{R_1}{R_1}) = \frac{R_1}{R_1 R_2} + \frac{R_1}{R_1 R_2} = \frac{R_1 + R_2}{R_1 R_2}$$

So, now we have:

$$\frac{1}{R_t} = \frac{R_1 + R_2}{R_1 R_2}. \text{ Inversing, } \quad \frac{R_t}{1} = \frac{R_1 R_2}{R_1 + R_2} = R_t$$

This derivation is for two resistors in parallel; for more resistors in parallel, the same derivation technique would be followed.

Given that all the resistors in a parallel circuit are of the same resistive value, the following is a short calculation of the total circuit resistance.

Take the resistive value of one of the resistors and divide it by the number of resistors in the parallel circuit. Assuming that 5 resistors are in parallel and each one is 500 ohms, to calculate the total circuit resistance, divide 500 by 5 and the result is 100 ohms.

An interesting aspect of resistance is that the inverse (1/R) is conduction, the ease with which electrons can flow through a given material, and is expressed in units of *mhos* with a symbol that is the same as the resistance symbol inverted.

The color codes for resistors are as follows:

2

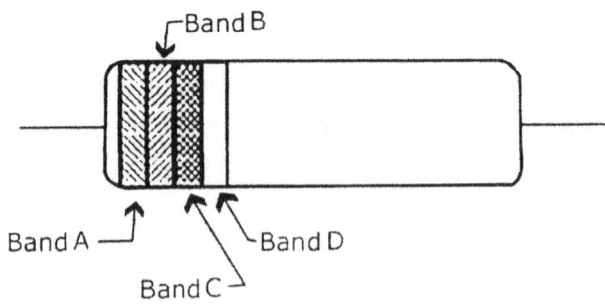

Band A is the first digit of the value of the resistor.
Band B is the second digit of the value of the resistor.
Band C is the decimal multiplier.
Band D is the tolerance of the value of the resistor.

The colors and their values are:

COLOR	VALUE	COLOR	VALUE	TOLERANCE COLORS
BLACK	0	GREEN	5	
BROWN	1	BLUE	6	GOLD 5%
RED	2	VIOLET	7	SILVER 10%
ORANGE	3	GRAY	8	NO COLOR 20%
YELLOW	4	WHITE	9	

So, a resistor colored as:
   1st band   violet
   2nd band   green
   3rd band   blue
   4th band   silver
is computed as:

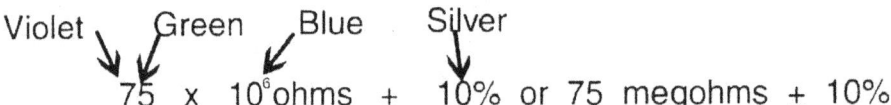

An easy way of remembering the sequence of the color codes above is to remember the following sentence and use the first letters of each word: *Bad Boys Race Our Young Girls Behind Victory Garden Walls*.

Ohms' Law

Ohm's law is the law that establishes the mathematical relationship of current, voltage, and resistance in a circuit. The formula is: $E = IR$, where E = the circuit or component voltage, I = the circuit or component current, and R = the circuit or component resistance.

In the circuit shown below, we know E = 10 volts and I=5 ohms. Deriving the formula, we get $I = E/R$. So, $I = 10/5 = 2$ amps.

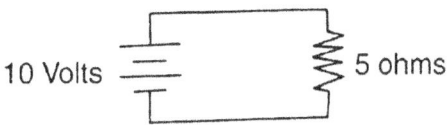

The power consumed by a component is equal to E x I. So, P = EI, and this calculated value is expressed in units of watts.

Kirchoff's Voltage Law

Kirchoff's voltage law states in technical terms that in a simple series circuit, as shown below, the algebraic sum of the voltages around the circuit is zero. Basically, this means that the supply voltage, Vsupply, is equal to VA + VB + VC, which are the voltage drops across the respective resistors in the circuit below. In the parallel circuit shown below, the voltages in each of the individual branches are equal to each other as well as equal to the total circuit voltage.

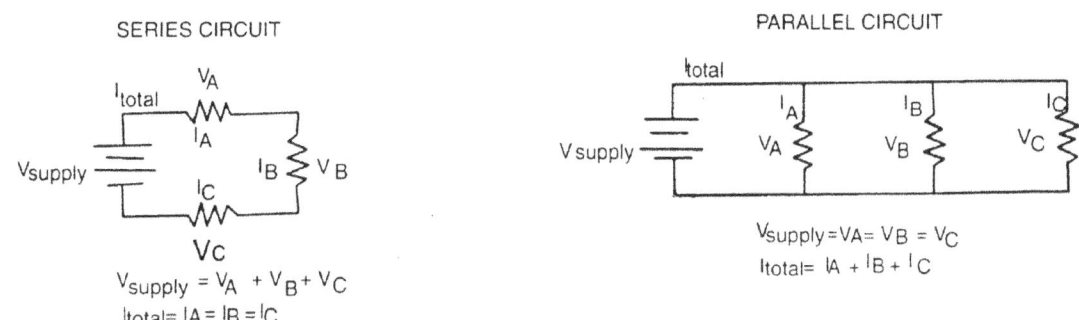

Kirchoff's Current Law

Kirchoff's current law states that at any junction of conductors in a circuit, the algebraic sum of the currents is zero. On a series circuit shown above, current is equal across each individual component as well as equal to the total circuit current. In a parallel circuit, the current across each individual branch when added is equal to the total circuit current, as in the parallel circuit shown above.

Inductors

Inductors are coils that oppose changes in current, which also store energy in a magnetic field. Induction is expressed in units of henries, and represented by an h. Inductance in series and parallel circuits is summed in the same manner as resistance. Inductors tend to block AC signals and pass DC voltages. An inductor's ability to oppose AC current is called inductive reactance. Inductive reactance is expressed in ohms just like resistance, but is represented by the symbol ZL, where Z means impedance and L added specifies inductive reactance or impedance. The impedance symbol Ω should not be confused with the resistive symbol, which is the same. The formula for inductive reactance is: $X_L = 2\pi fL$, where $\pi = 3.14$, f = the frequency of the AC signal to be used, and L = the inductance in henries. The schematic symbol for an inductor is

Adding two lines on the top of the symbol means that it is an iron core filled inductor. Since they have a magnetic field, they are used in transformers and electromagnetic switches.

Capacitors

Capacitors consist basically of two metal plates in parallel separated by an insulator (dielectric). Capacitors have the ability to store a charge in an electrostatic field between its two plates. This charge is dependent upon two things, the capacitance of the circuit and the difference in the potential of the circuit. The capacitance of a capacitor is measured in farads, and is depicted by the letter C. Capacitance is summed in a manner that is exactly opposite to that of resistors, since it is directly summed when in parallel as shown below.

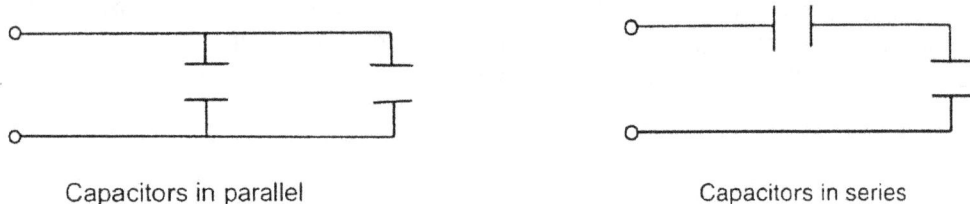

Capacitors in parallel   Capacitors in series

In the parallel circuit shown above, if one of the capacitors is 1 farad and the other is 2 farads, then total circuit capacitance is 3 farads. Capacitance of such a high value is rare and usually limited to industrial use. More realistic values would be in the microfarad range. When capacitors are in series as shown above, they are added, as are resistors in parallel. So, the formula would be: $Ct = \dfrac{C_1 C_2}{C_1 + C_2}$

As with inductors, capacitors are also measured by the opposition that they may give to AC current flow, which is called capacitive reactance. Capacitive reactance, X_c, is expressed also in units of ohms, and its formula is:

$$X_c = \frac{1}{2\Pi fC}$$

where f = the frequency in hertz of the AC signal, and C = the capacitance, in farads. Electrolytic capacitors are polarized, which means that they must be placed in circuits with polarity considerations.

AC Cycles

The five main forms of AC signals are sawtooth, sinusoidal, square, rectangular, and trapezoidal waveforms.

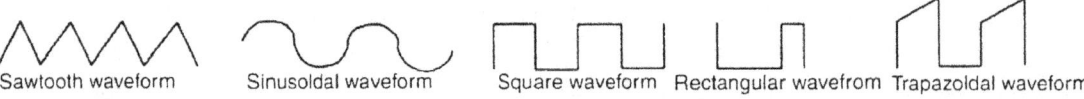

Sawtooth waveform   Sinusoidal waveform   Square waveform   Rectangular wavefrom   Trapazoldal waveform

There are also parts of sinewaves that are of interest.

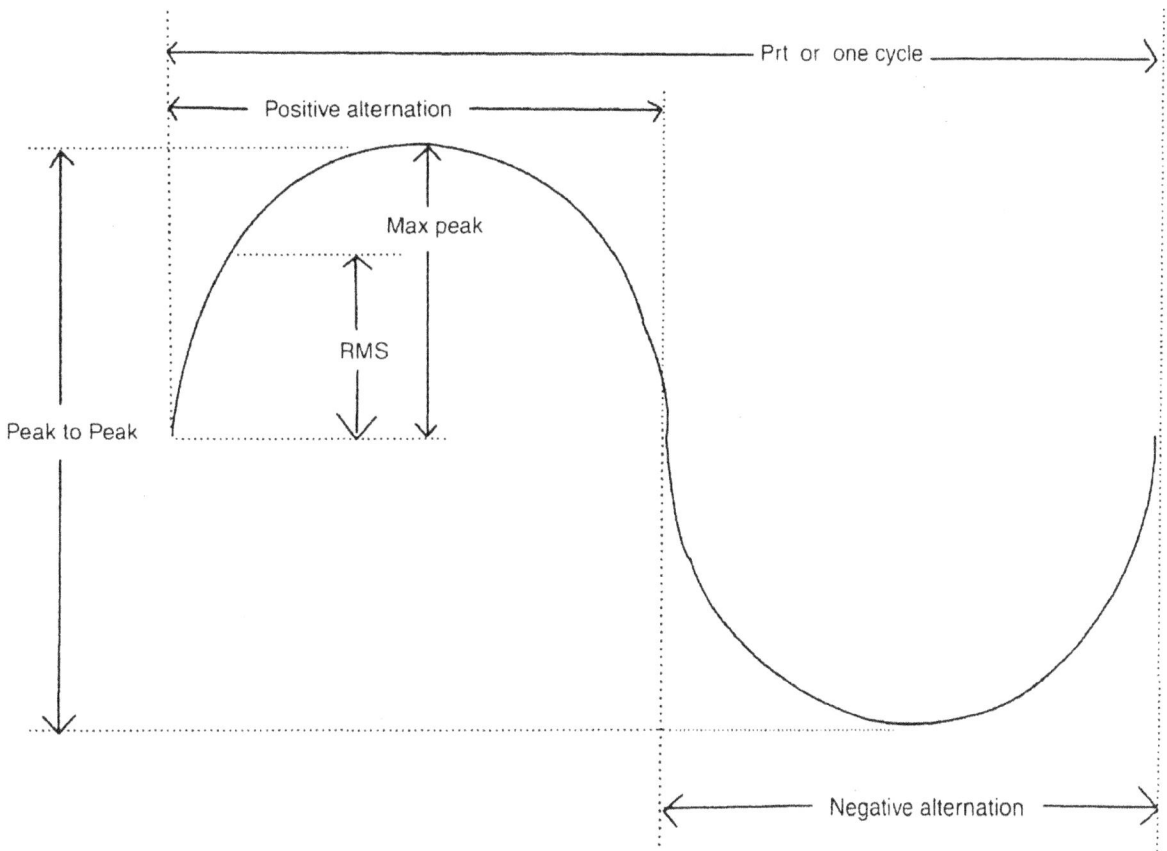

The RMS value (root mean square) is the same as the effective value, which is the value of an AC signal that has the same power or heating effect as a DC voltage. With sinusoidal waveforms, this value is equal to .707 times the AC voltage peak.

The average value is the value of an AC signal of a positive alternation and in a sinusoidal waveform is equal to .637 times the maximum voltage or peak.

Magnetism

The basic properties of magnetism are permeability, reluctance, and retentivity.

Permeability is the property of the ease with which a metal will allow magnetic lines of flux to pass through it.

Reluctance is a property of a metal that opposes lines of flux going through it.

Retentivity is the ability of a magnetized metal to stay magnetized.

Permanent magnets have high retentivity. Steel has high retentivity, low permeability, and high reluctance. Soft iron has low retentivity, high permeability, and low reluctance.

When a wire has current passing through it, the wire will have an electromagnetic field around it. The left hand rule can be used to determine the direction of the electromagnetic lines. To do this, place your left hand with fingers wrapped around the wire and your thumb pointed in the direction of current flow. The direction in which your fingers are pointing is the direction of the electromagnetic lines of flux.

Relays

The three types of relays are power relays, control relays, and sensing relays. Power relays control high voltages going to circuits such as motors. Control relays are used to energize and de-energize other relays and associated circuitry. Sensing relays are used to detect such items as over or under, current or voltages. When sensed by the sensing relay, power sources will be disconnected.

Switches

The various types of switches are identified by the number of poles, throws, and positions that they have. The number of *poles* that a switch has indicates the number of terminals through which voltages may enter the switch. The number of *throws* refers to the number of circuits that could be completed or disconnected by each blade or contacter. The number of *positions* indicates the number of different places that the toggle of the switch can be placed in.
The four kinds of switches are shown below.

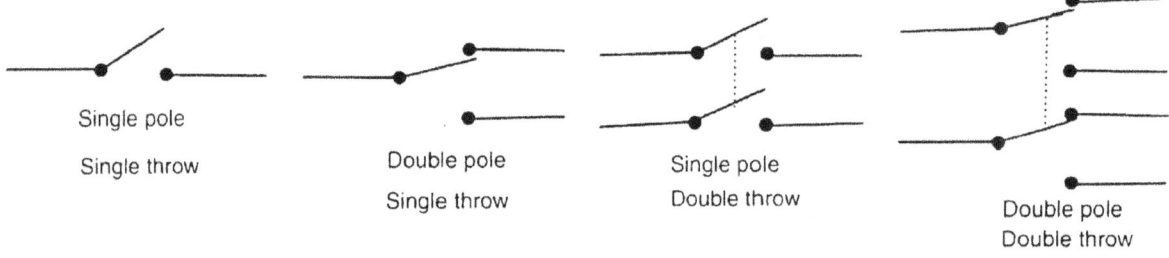

Single pole
Single throw

Double pole
Single throw

Single pole
Double throw

Double pole
Double throw

Diodes

As its name implies, a simple rectifier diode is used for signal rectification. The schematic symbol is shown below. Zener diodes are designed for specific reverse breakdown voltages; and since they keep the voltage across the diode constant, they are used for voltage regulation. Tunnel diodes will give negative resistance for specific ranges of forward bias voltages. Because of this phenomenon, tunnel diodes are used as amplifiers or oscillators. Silicon controlled rectifiers (SCR) are triggered diodes. These are used to control AC voltages on one particular half cycle. Diacs work on both sides of the cycles of an AC signal. Triacs are gated diacs. Basically, SCRs, diacs, and triacs are used to pick out desired portions of AC signals.

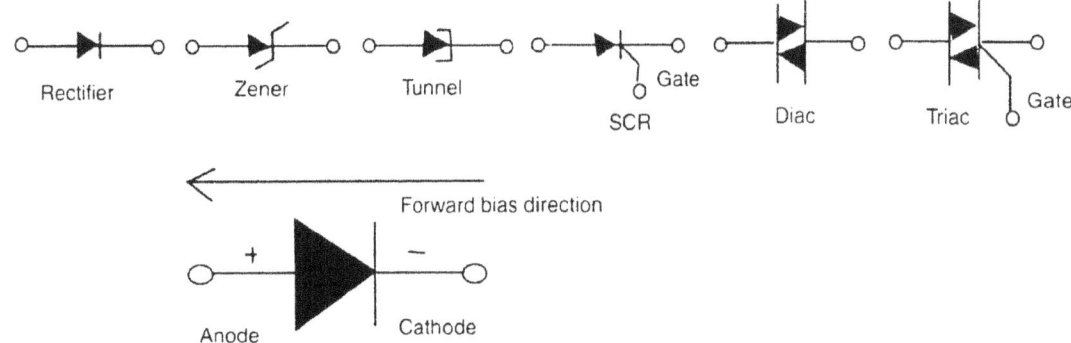

Transistors

Transistors are solid state devices that can act as amplifiers or switches. They are classified as bipolar and field-effect transistors. The bipolar transistor allows current flow in either direction. The two types of bipolar transistors are PNP and NPN transistors, which are shown below.

When used strictly as a switch, the PNP transistor requires a negative input signal on the base to turn it on or conduct. Conversely, the NPN transistor requires a positive signal on the base to turn it on.

Bipolar transistors are not only used as switches and have several configurations. The different transistor configurations and their respective traits are shown below:

<u>BEG</u>
VPI
ABG
LMH
HML
IOI

The <u>first</u> line is the type of configuration, i.e., common base, emitter, or collector. The particular transistor's configuration traits are shown vertically below the transistor. Line <u>two</u> shows electrical gains (voltage, power, or current). Line <u>three</u> shows the type of gain (alpha, beta, or gamma). Line <u>four</u> shows the input impedance of the configuration (low, medium, or high). Line <u>five</u> shows the output impedance (high, medium, or low).

Line <u>six</u> shows the output signal phase relationship with the input (in-phase or out-of-phase).

There are two types of field effect transistors (FET) - JFETs and MOSFETs. <u>JFETs</u> stand for junction field transistors and control large voltages with very small inputs and, therefore, can be used as amplifiers. <u>MOSFETs</u> stands for metal-oxide-semiconductor field effect transistors and have a higher input impedance and can use even smaller signals. They are also smaller and are configured by the thousands to form chips.

<u>Soldering</u>

Electrical connections are joined by soldering. Soldering requires a high heat source and an alloy that melts at a relatively low temperature when compared to other metals. The basic soldering technique is to first heat the joint to be soldered with a soldering device and then place the solder directly onto the joint with the soldering device still in contact. Allow the solder to melt and flow onto the joint surface covering the joint area. Once this occurs, remove solder and device, allowing to cool without any movement of the joint area. After the solder hardens, inspect the solder joint. The joint should look smooth, bright, and shiny, with the surface area of the joint smoothly covered. If the solder has the appearance of being partially balled up instead of a smooth semi-flat flow, it is called a *cold solder* joint. A possible cause of a cold solder joint might be wrongly applying the solder to the solder device and then dropping onto the area to be soldered. If the solder joint is not shiny but dull and gray instead, then the connection was probably moved prior to the solder hardening completely.

Solder is an alloy usually made up of various ratios and combinations of tin and lead. Some that are resin filled are also called flux. Soldering fluxes are used to de-oxide surfaces that are being soldered. One type of flux is acid-core resin, which is very corrosive to electrical connections and should be avoided.

Soldering devices come in various sizes, depending on the job required to be done. One of the most delicate of soldering jobs, soldering components with very small connections onto printed circuit boards, is usually done by pencil irons. These miniature irons are ideal for providing low heat to small areas. Soldering jobs that require more heat use items such as solder guns. These produce high heat and heat up very quickly.

The types of solder tips most commonly used in electrical work are made of copper or copper alloys, since copper has high heat conductivity and good tinning quality. The tinning of a soldering tip increases heat transfer/conductivity to the area to be soldered and also reduces scaling of the solder tip. Tinning consists of getting a good layer of solder on the working surface of the copper tip. Cleaning tips that become dirty or discolored requires dipping the tip in water while hot, and quickly removing it or wiping with a damp sponge or towel.

II. COMPUTERS

The 5 major components of a computer are input, storage, control unit, arithmetic and "logic unit, and output. The <u>input</u> device allows information such as data and commands or instructions to be fed into the computer system. The most common type of input device is the keyboard. Other input devices are magnetic and optical readers. <u>Storage</u> devices are used to store memory, such as instructions or data until they are needed. Memory is stored in bits, which is the most basic element of binary numbers, a 1 or 0. Bytes are groups of eight bits. A nibble is half of a byte. The <u>control unit</u> coordinates the operations of the entire computer. It interprets programs and issues instructions to accomplish the program. The <u>output</u> device communicates the progress or results of a program used in the computer to the operator/user. The devices range from monitor screens to high speed printers.

Numbering Systems

Computers and associated circuitry use several numbering systems that have different bases. We are all familiar with base 10 numbering system. This is the system we use in everyday life. In this system, each decimal/digit place represents a value of 10, whether it is the first digit to the left of the decimal point, which is a 10 to the 0 power or one's. The second digit to the left represents the number of 10's and the third represents the number of 100's.

The other base sytems work in the same fashion with their own respective bases. The other base systems used are base 2 (binary), base 8 (octal), and base 16 (hexadecimal). It is easy to convert from one system to another.

	5th digit	4th digit	3rd digit	2nd digit	1st digit
Base 10	10^4	10^3	10^2	10^1	10^0
Base 2	2^4	2^3	2^2	2^1	2^0
Base 8	8^4	8^3	8^2	8^1	8^0
Base 16	16^4	16^3	16^2	16^1	16^0

The largest number in base 10 is a 9, for base 2 it is 1, for base 8 it is 7, for base 16 it is 15. The numbers for base 16 greater than 9 are expressed by letters, i.e., 10 = A, 11 = B, 12 = C, 13 = D, 14 = E, and 15 = F.

The following is a conversion of the base 16 number to the other bases. The number will be $2B7_{16}$

```
     2      B*      7
   x16      +       +     Base 16    So 2B7₁₆ = 695₁₀
   ---     32     688
    32     ---    ---
           43     695                *B = 11
            x
           16
           ---
           688
```

The procedure for calculating is to start with the most significant digit and multiply it by the value base used. In this case, the most significant digit is a 2 and the base value is 16. Next, take the result of the multiplication and add this to the next lower digit and then multiply by the digit place value. This was (32+11) x 16 = 688. This procedure continues until the least significant digit is reached. At this point, just add the accumulated value so far with the last digit.

This same process is used for converting any other number of a different base to base 10 number, using the respective base values.

To convert a base 10 number to its base 16 (or any base), the process is as follows: First, the base 10 number is divided by the base number of the base system it is to be converted to. To reconvert 695 base 10 back to base 16, 695/16 = 43 with a remainder of 7. The remainder (7) is the least significant digit of the new base number. Next, 43/16 = 2 with a remainder of 11. 11 is the next digit because we are going to base 16, 11 = B. Since it is less than the base number (16), 2 becomes the most significant digit. So, the converted number is 2B7 base 16.

To convert the base 10 number to base 8, 695/8 = 86 with a remainder of 7, which will be the least significant digit. Now, 86/8 = 10 with a remainder of 6, which is the next digit. Finally, 10/8 = 1 with a remainder of 2, which is the next digit. 1 is left as the most significant digit. So, 695 base 10 = 1267 base 8.

We can reverse this to see if it is correct. Multiply the most significant digit 1 by 8. 1x8=8. Add this to the next digit and multiply by 8, (8+2) x 8 = 80. Add the result to the next digit and multiply by 8, (80+6) x 8 = 688. Now, add the result to the last (least significant) digit, 688 + 7 = 695. So, 695 base 10 does = 1267 base 8.

Performing base 2 calculations is just as simple. Take 21 base 10 and convert to base 2. 21/2 = 10 with a remainder of 1, which is the least significant digit. 10/2 = 5 with a remainder of 0, which will be the next digit. 5/2= 2 with a remainder of 1, the next digit. 2/2 = 1 with a remainder of 0, the next digit. The remaining number will be the next most significant digit. So, 23 base 10 = 10101 base 2.

Reverse this to check: 1x2=2. (2+0) x 2 = 4. (4+1) x 2 = 10. (10+0) x 2 = 20. (20+1) = 21. So, 23 base 10 does equal 10101 base 2.

Flip Flops

Flip flops have one of two stable states. They change states by receiving input pulses. The reset-set flip flop (RS FF) is one of the most basic forms of flip flops made by interconnecting two NAND gates.

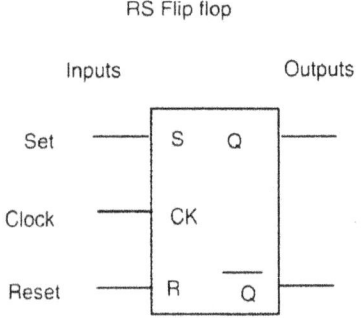

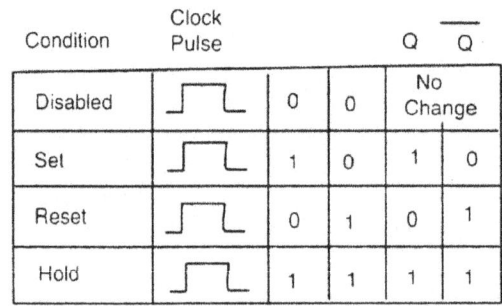

Condition	Clock Pulse			Q	Q̄
Disabled	⎍	0	0	No Change	
Set	⎍	1	0	1	0
Reset	⎍	0	1	0	1
Hold	⎍	1	1	1	1

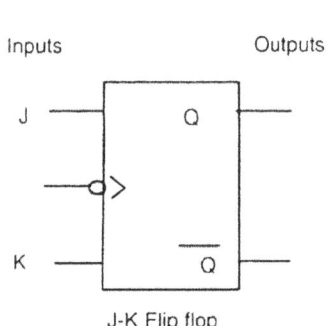

Condition	Clock Pulse	J	K	Q	Q̄
Hold	⎍	0	0	NO Change	
Set	⎍	1	0	1	0
Reset	⎍	0	1	0	1
Toggle	⎍	1	1	Change to Opposite state	

J-K Flip flop

A flip flop with a clock input is called a synchronous device; without a clock input it is called an asynchronous device.

The most common type of flip flop is the J-K flop flip (shown on the previous page). The J + K inputs are data inputs. The arrowhead > at the clock input means that the flip flop is edge triggered. The bubble 0 means that the flip flop is negative edge triggered. Flip flops can be put together to make counters such as:

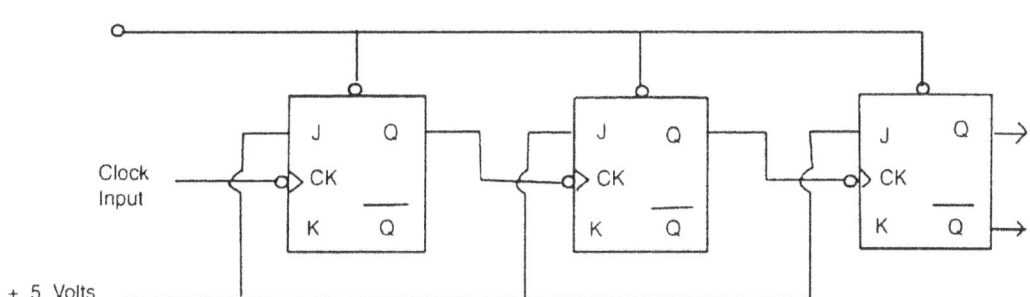

Shift registers also use flip flops in which data is loaded serially (one bit at a time). Once the FF's are loaded with data, they can be shifted left or right (depending upon how they are wired), by clock pulses. Shifting the data to the left or right will either divide by 2 or multiply by 2, depending on which FF has the least significant digit.

The following represent adders which perform arithmetic operations:

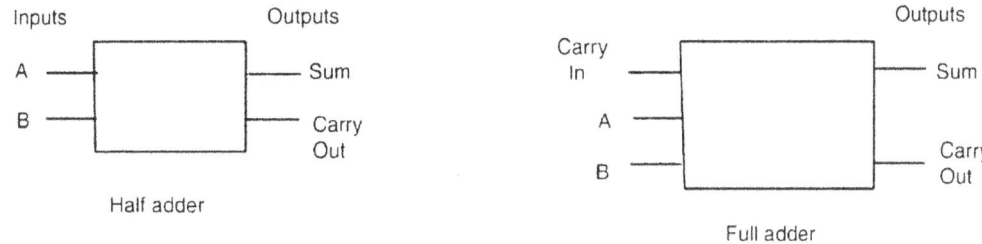

Half adders add binary numbers like the full adder, but do not consider previous carry inputs.

The significance of flip flops is that they can be grouped together to form units of memory, such as RAMs, ROMs, PROMs, and EPROMs. RAM (random access memory) is volatile memory, meaning that when power is turned off, the stored memory is lost. RAM is considered a read-write memory, meaning that you can read data from or write data into the memory. ROM (read-only memory) is non-volatile, meaning that when power is turned off, memory is not lost. ROMs are permanently programmed by the manufacturer and is often called firmware. PROMs (programmable read-only memory) are special ROMs designed to allow the user to program the ROM. EPROMs (erasable programmable read-only memory) are also special ROMs that allow the user to program memories and erase the programs.

Logic Gates

Logic gates use binary inputs. In positive logic, a 1 is a high input and a 0 is a low input. In negative logic, a 1 is a low input and a 0 is a high input.

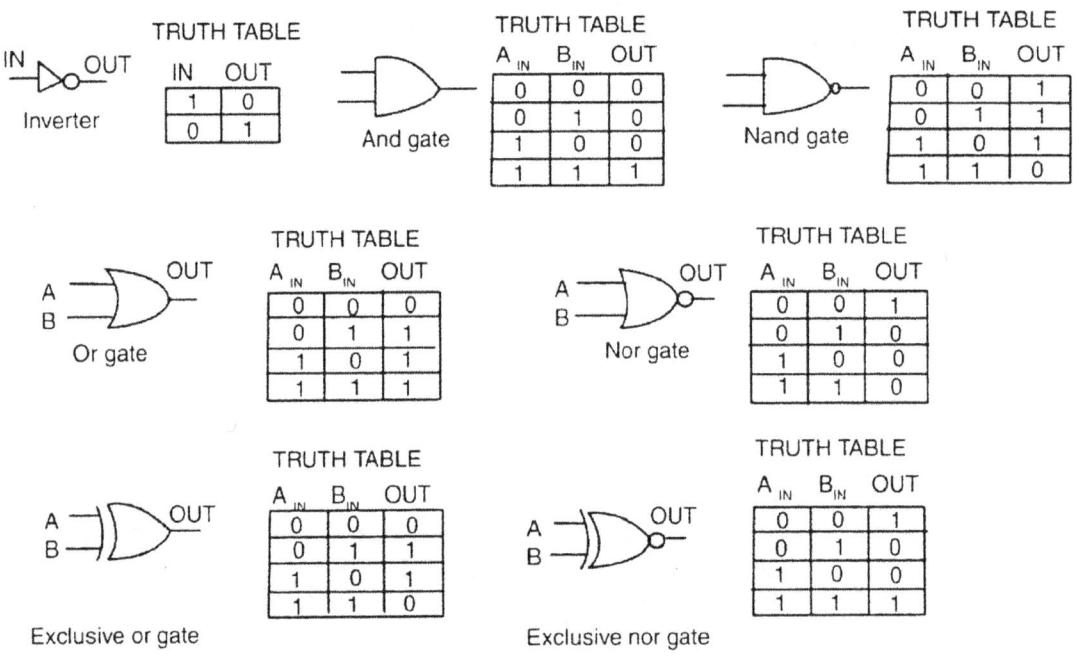

III. OSCILLOSCOPES

Oscilloscopes are used to display instantaneous voltage waveforms in graphic form. The display screen is set up and divided vertically and horizontally in 1 cm divisions. There are 8 vertical divisions in which waveform amplitude is displayed and 10 horizontal divisions in which the time of the wavelength is displayed.

The VOLTS/DIV knob allows the user to select the waveform voltage amplitude in each vertical division to be displayed. The SEC/DIV knob allows the user to select the sweep speed of the waveform in each horizontal division to be displayed.

Proper use of the oscilloscope requires the ability to analyze displayed waveforms by observing the number of divisions a cycle of a given waveform covers both vertically and horizontally.

13

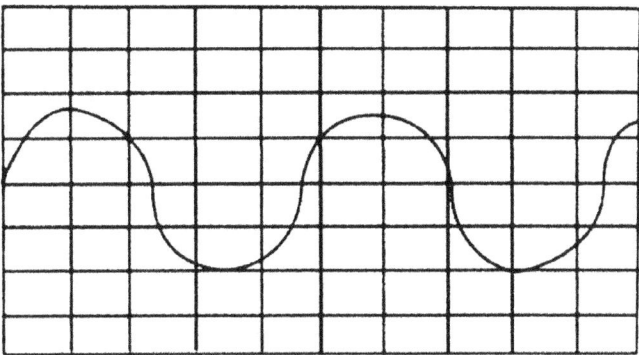

In the waveform shown above, the VOLT/DIV knob is set on 5 volts/div and the SEC/DIV knob is set to 1 msec/div.

Count the number of divisions covered vertically by the waveform, which is 3 1/2 divisions. To get the actual peak-to-peak amplitude of the sinewave, perform the following calculation: 3 1/2 divisions x 5 volts/division = 17.5 volts peak to peak.

Now count the number of divisions covered horizontally by one complete cycle of the waveform, which in this case is 4 1/2 divisions. To find the PRT (pulse repetition time), perform the following calculation: 4 1/2 divisions x .001 sec/division = .0045 seconds. .0045 seconds x msec/.001 sec = 4.5 msec for the PRT.

To find the frequency, simply invert the PRT: Frequency = 1/PRT = 1/.0045 sec = 222.22 cycles/sec or hertz.

The same process could be reversed to find the settings to use on an oscilloscope when you know the amplitude and frequency of a given waveform/signal that you would like to view on the oscilloscope.

<u>Meters</u>

The following are the basics of measuring meters: Always measure current *in series* with the circuit to be measured and always measure voltage in parallel with the circuit.

When performing resistance measurements, always ensure that the component or circuit has no voltage on it and consider whether a specific component may need to be isolated from the rest of the circuit so that the resistance measurement does not follow an alternate path. This can be accomplished by removing one of the *electrical* legs of the component from the circuit. When unsure of the amount of voltage on a circuit to be measured, start with the highest meter setting or range.

When using analog or needle deflection type meters, ensure that you have the proper polarity of leads when checking for DC voltages. One of the most popular analog type multimeters used is the Simpson 260. For copyright reasons, a copy of the meter cannot be given but here are some tips that will work using any analog multimeter. When performing DC measurements, look at the range setting that you have the meter set up for, and find the same corresponding scale on the meter face for proper readings. When performing resistance measurements, read the resistance value on the resistance scale where the needle is deflected to and then multiply this by the resistance range setting. An example of this is with the needle setting on a value of 8 on the resistance scale and the range knob on *RX1000*, then the value of resistance is 8000 ohms.

IV. SCIENTIFIC NOTATION

Scientific notation is a way of expressing large numbers. For example, 100,000,000 ohms could be written as 100×10^6 ohms or 100 megohms. Other prefixes like meg are listed below.

FACTOR	PREFIX	SYMBOL	FACTOR	PREFIX	SYMBOL
10^{12}	tera	T	10^{-2}	centi	c
10^9	giga	G	10^{-3}	milli	m
10^6	mega	M	10^{-6}	micro	μ
10^3	kilo	K	10^{-9}	nano	n
10^2	hecto	h	10^{-12}	pico	p
10^1	deka	da	10^{-15}	femto	f
10^{-1}	deci	d	10^{-18}	atto	a

V. GEARS

Gears are wheels with teeth that are used to transmit mechanical motion from one point to another. The usual configuration is that of two gears meshed together. In this configuration, the larger gear is simply called a *gear* and the smaller gear is called a *pinion*. If the pinion drives the gear, the system is called a speed reducer. If the gear drives the pinion, then the system is called a speed increaser.

When gears are used in increasing or decreasing speeds, they are configured in gear ratios. This allows specific speed changes. For example, for a gear to turn 100 revolutions per minute, if the shaft of the driving motor turns at 1000 revolutions per minute, to achieve the desired speed, it is necessary to use a reducer configuration. This is accomplished by changing the gear ratios. Since gears are made with a certain number of teeth per inch, reducing the number of teeth per inch on the gear attached to the motor shaft to one-tenth of that of the other gear that is being driven would reduce the speed of the driving shaft from 1000 revolutions per minute to 100 revolutions per minute on the driven shaft.

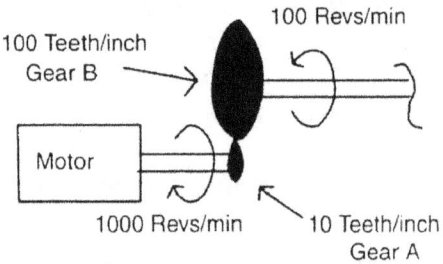

The basic formula for calculating the relationship between the gears and their respective speeds is: Revs/min(gear A) x Teeth/inch (gear A) = Revs/min(gear B) x Teeth/inch(gear B).

When two gears mesh, they turn in opposite directions. Adding a third gear called an idler gear and placing it in-between the two gears will allow them to turn in the same direction. There are four basic types of gear configurations, and they are spur, worm, helical/herringbone, and bevel gears.

<u>Spur gears</u> are the most common type, having straight teeth. They are used to transmit power between two parallel shafts.

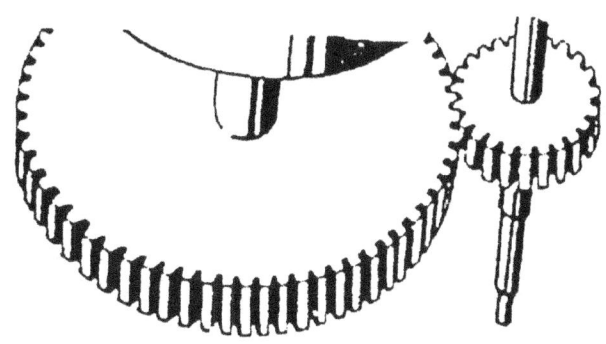

TYPICAL SPUR GEAR

<u>Worm gears</u> having helical teeth are used to transmit power between two shafts whose axis intersect, but not in the same plane. This is probably the most common method of speed reduction, especially in conveyers because the speed of a very fast rotating motor can be greatly reduced.

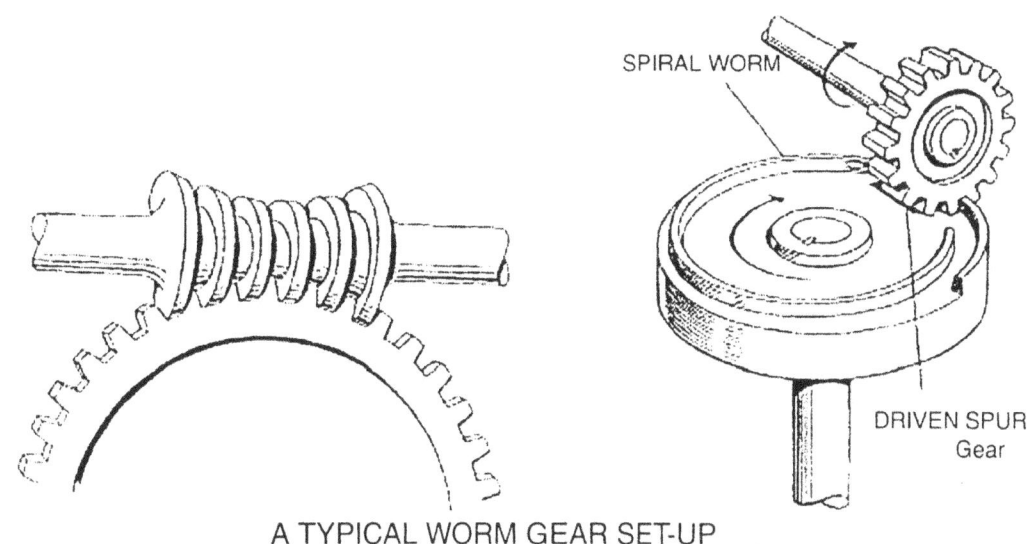

A TYPICAL WORM GEAR SET-UP

<u>Helical/herringbone gears</u> have spiral teeth which allows them to transmit power between two shafts at any angle.

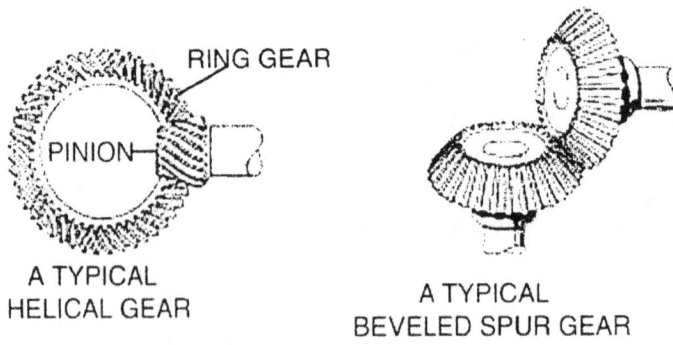

A TYPICAL HELICAL GEAR

A TYPICAL BEVELED SPUR GEAR

Bevel gears are shaped like sections of cones and used to transmit power between shafts whose axis intersect.

Pulleys

Pulleys are wheels used to transmit power such as pulleys used to transmit power from a motor to drive the roller of a conveyer belt. The main feature of a pulley is its ability to change speeds or revolutions per minute. When a pulley drives another pulley with a smaller diameter, the rpms of the second pulley will be greater. This results in a speed increase similar to that in gear systems.

A formula for calculating the circumference around a pulley is: $C = 2\pi r$, where r is the radius of the pulley, and $\pi = 3.14$. Through a series of derivations, the relationship of respective rpms between two connected pulleys is as follows.
Arpms = Brpms x rB/rA where:
  Arpms = revolutions per minute of pulley A
  Brpms = revolutions per minute of pulley B
  rB = radius of pulley B
  rA = radius of pulley A

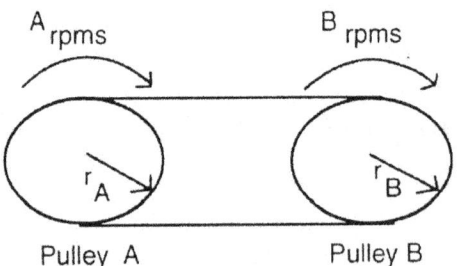

Pulley A   Pulley B

Another use of pulleys is compounding. Compound bows used for archery take advantage of the physics involved in compounding to allow archers to draw bows at high weight pulls with relative ease. For example, to pull up a 100 lb. weight, instead of having to pull with a force of 100 lbs., pulleys can be used to lessen the force required.

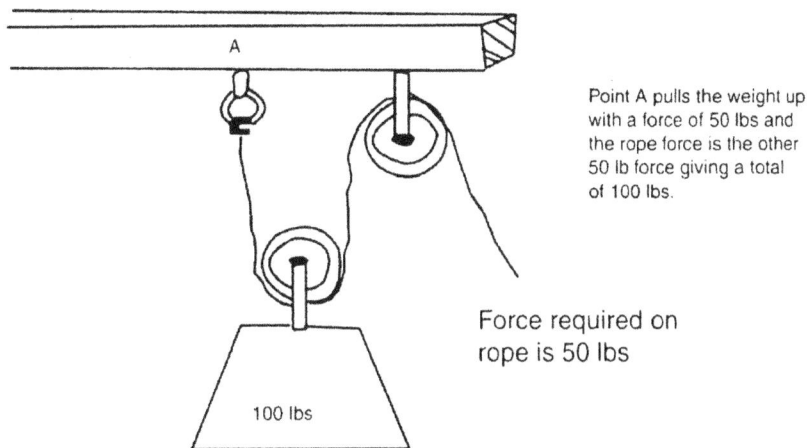

Point A pulls the weight up with a force of 50 lbs and the rope force is the other 50 lb force giving a total of 100 lbs.

Force required on rope is 50 lbs

A pawl is a device used to allow a wheel to turn in one direction and lock the wheel from turning in the other direction. Pawls are commonly found in winching or come-along set-ups.

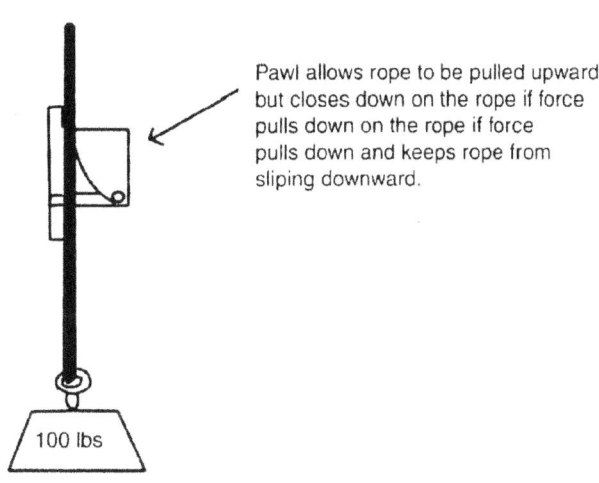

Pawl allows rope to be pulled upward, but closes down on the rope if force pulls down on the rope if force pulls down and keeps rope from sliping downward.

Special coupling is required in power transmissions in order to get mechanical power from one point to another. There are four general types of coupling. The first type is rigid coupling and is rarely used because the shafts must be exactly parallel and, therefore, do not allow for misalignment. The second is flexible coupling which allows for some misalignment although excessive misalignment increases wear. The third type is chain coupling which has been mostly replaced by flexible coupling which requires the most maintenance of all couplings. The last is fluid coupling which uses steel shot as a flow charge. This allows the motor to pick up loads gradually.

Chains should be mounted horizontally or not more than 60 degrees off the horizontal plane. They do allow for the most misalignment. Hook-shaped sprocket teeth show excessive wear. Misalignment may be identified by inspecting for wear on the sides of teeth on the inner surface of roller link plates. The chain sag should not be greater than 2% of the distances from the sprockets, which is 1/4 inch per foot.

A cam is a device connected to a rotating shaft used to convert rotary motion into reciprocal motion.

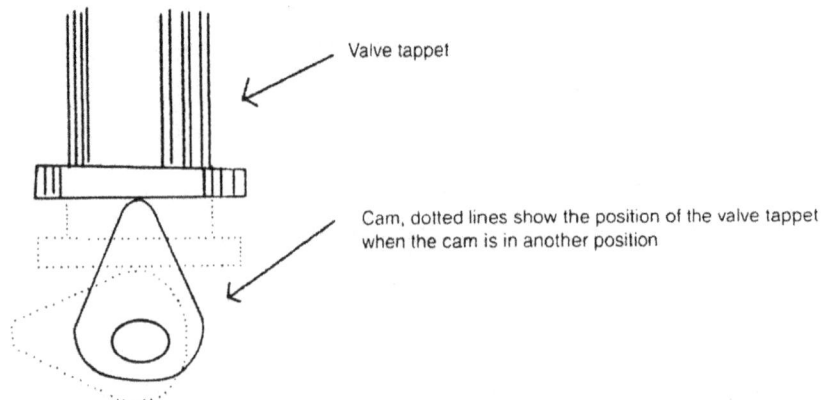

Valve tappet

Cam, dotted lines show the position of the valve tappet when the cam is in another position

Lubricants

Lubrication materials occur in many mediums. Three that will be discussed here are oils, greases, and solids.

Multigrade oils are the most versatile of the oil types. They have additives that allow them to be used in a wide range of temperatures. For example, in an oil labeled 10 w/30, 10 is the SAE viscosity number at 0 degrees Fahrenheit, and the SAE viscosity number at 210 degrees Fahrenheit is 30.

Greases are used in the lubrication of ball or idler bearing systems. Generally speaking, greases are oils that have had thickening agents or *soaps* added. The different kinds of greases are graded from 000, which is a *semi-fluid*, to 6 which is described as being very stiff or thick.

Another type of lubricant is solids. The most common type of solid lubricant is graphite. Another type is molybdenumdisulphide. Solid lubricants are extremely useful as anti-seize compounds to protect rubbing surfaces under high pressures and temperatures from metal pick-up.

ELECTRICAL TERMS AND FORMULAS

CONTENTS

	Page
TERMS	1
Agonic ...... Dielectric	1
Diode ...... Lead	2
Line of Force ...... Resistor	3
Retentivity ...... Wattmeter	4
FORMULAS	4
Ohm's Law for D-C Circuits	4
Resistors in Series	4
Resistors in Parallel	4
R-L Circuit Time Constant	5
R-C Circuit Time Constant	5
Comparison of Units in Electric and Magnetic Circuits	5
Capacitors in Series	5
Capacitors in Parallel	5
Capacitive Reactance	5
Impedance in an R-C Circuit (Series)	5
Inductors in Series	5
Inductors in Parallel	5
Inductive Reactance	5
Q of a Coil	5
Impedance of an R-L Circuit (Series)	5
Impedance with R, C, and L in Series	5
Parallel Circuit Impedance	5
Sine-Wave Voltage Relationships	5
Power in A-C Circuit	6
Transformers	6
Three-Phase Voltage and Current Relationships	6
GREEK ALPHABET	7
Alpha ...... Omega	7
COMMON ABBREVIATIONS AND LETTER SYMBOLS	8
Alternating Current (noun) ...... Watt	8

ELECTRICAL TERMS AND FORMULAS

Terms

AGONIC.—An imaginary line of the earth's surface passing through points where the magnetic declination is 0°; that is, points where the compass points to true north.

AMMETER.—An instrument for measuring the amount of electron flow in amperes.

AMPERE.—The basic unit of electrical current.

AMPERE-TURN.—The magnetizing force produced by a current of one ampere flowing through a coil of one turn.

AMPLIDYNE.—A rotary magnetic or dynamoelectric amplifier used in servomechanism and control applications.

AMPLIFICATION.—The process of increasing the strength (current, power, or voltage) of a signal.

AMPLIFIER.—A device used to increase the signal voltage, current, or power, generally composed of a vacuum tube and associated circuit called a stage. It may contain several stages in order to obtain a desired gain.

AMPLITUDE.—The maximum instantaneous value of an alternating voltage or current, measured in either the positive or negative direction.

ARC.—A flash caused by an electric current ionizing a gas or vapor.

ARMATURE.—The rotating part of an electric motor or generator. The moving part of a relay or vibrator.

ATTENUATOR.—A network of resistors used to reduce voltage, current, or power delivered to a load.

AUTOTRANSFORMER.—A transformer in which the primary and secondary are connected together in one winding.

BATTERY.—Two or more primary or secondary cells connected together electrically. The term does not apply to a single cell.

BREAKER POINTS.—Metal contacts that open and close a circuit at timed intervals.

BRIDGE CIRCUIT.—The electrical bridge circuit is a term referring to any one of a variety of electric circuit networks, one branch of which, the "bridge" proper, connects two points of equal potential and hence carries no current when the circuit is properly adjusted or balanced.

BRUSH.—The conducting material, usually a block of carbon, bearing against the commutator or sliprings through which the current flows in or out.

BUS BAR.—A primary power distribution point connected to the main power source.

CAPACITOR.—Two electrodes or sets of electrodes in the form of plates, separated from each other by an insulating material called the dielectric.

CHOKE COIL.—A coil of low ohmic resistance and high impedance to alternating current.

CIRCUIT.—The complete path of an electric current.

CIRCUIT BREAKER.—An electromagnetic or thermal device that opens a circuit when the current in the circuit exceeds a predetermined amount. Circuit breakers can be reset.

CIRCULAR MIL.—An area equal to that of a circle with a diameter of 0.001 inch. It is used for measuring the cross section of wires.

COAXIAL CABLE.—A transmission line consisting of two conductors concentric with and insulated from each other.

COMMUTATOR.—The copper segments on the armature of a motor or generator. It is cylindrical in shape and is used to pass power into or from the brushes. It is a switching device.

CONDUCTANCE.—The ability of a material to conduct or carry an electric current. It is the reciprocal of the resistance of the material, and is expressed in mhos.

CONDUCTIVITY.—The ease with which a substance transmits electricity.

CONDUCTOR.—Any material suitable for carrying electric current.

CORE.—A magnetic material that affords an easy path for magnetic flux lines in a coil.

COUNTER E.M.F.—Counter electromotive force; an e.m.f. induced in a coil or armature that opposes the applied voltage.

CURRENT LIMITER.—A protective device similar to a fuse, usually used in high amperage circuits.

CYCLE.—One complete positive and one complete negative alternation of a current or voltage.

DIELECTRIC.—An insulator; a term that refers to the insulating material between the plates of a capacitor.

ELECTRICAL TERMS AND FORMULAS

DIODE.—Vacuum tube—a two element tube that contains a cathode and plate; semiconductor—a material of either germanium or silicon that is manufactured to allow current to flow in only one direction. Diodes are used as rectifiers and detectors.

DIRECT CURRENT.—An electric current that flows in one direction only.

EDDY CURRENT.—Induced circulating currents in a conducting material that are caused by a varying magnetic field.

EFFICIENCY.—The ratio of output power to input power, generally expressed as a percentage.

ELECTROLYTE.—A solution of a substance which is capable of conducting electricity. An electrolyte may be in the form of either a liquid or a paste.

ELECTROMAGNET.—A magnet made by passing current through a coil of wire wound on a soft iron core.

ELECTROMOTIVE FORCE (e.m.f.).—The force that produces an electric current in a circuit.

ELECTRON.—A negatively charged particle of matter.

ENERGY.—The ability or capacity to do work.

FARAD.—The unit of capacitance.

FEEDBACK.—A transfer of energy from the output circuit of a device back to its input.

FIELD.—The space containing electric or magnetic lines of force.

FIELD WINDING.—The coil used to provide the magnetizing force in motors and generators.

FLUX FIELD.—All electric or magnetic lines of force in a given region.

FREE ELECTRONS.—Electrons which are loosely held and consequently tend to move at random among the atoms of the material.

FREQUENCY.—The number of complete cycles per second existing in any form of wave motion; such as the number of cycles per second of an alternating current.

FULL-WAVE RECTIFIER CIRCUIT.—A circuit which utilizes both the positive and the negative alternations of an alternating current to produce a direct current.

FUSE.—A protective device inserted in series with a circuit. It contains a metal that will melt or break when current is increased beyond a specific value for a definite period of time.

GAIN.—The ratio of the output power, voltage, or current to the input power, voltage, or current, respectively.

GALVANOMETER.—An instrument used to measure small d-c currents.

GENERATOR.—A machine that converts mechanical energy into electrical energy.

GROUND.—A metallic connection with the earth to establish ground potential. Also, a common return to a point of zero potential. The chassis of a receiver or a transmitter is sometimes the common return, and therefore the ground of the unit.

HENRY.—The basic unit of inductance.

HORSEPOWER.—The English unit of power, equal to work done at the rate of 550 foot-pounds per second. Equal to 746 watts of electrical power.

HYSTERESIS.—A lagging of the magnetic flux in a magnetic material behind the magnetizing force which is producing it.

IMPEDANCE.—The total opposition offered to the flow of an alternating current. It may consist of any combination of resistance, inductive reactance, and capacitive reactance.

INDUCTANCE.—The property of a circuit which tends to oppose a change in the existing current.

INDUCTION.—The act or process of producing voltage by the relative motion of a magnetic field across a conductor.

INDUCTIVE REACTANCE.—The opposition to the flow of alternating or pulsating current caused by the inductance of a circuit. It is measured in ohms.

INPHASE.—Applied to the condition that exists when two waves of the same frequency pass through their maximum and minimum values of like polarity at the same instant.

INVERSELY.—Inverted or reversed in position or relationship.

ISOGONIC LINE.—An imaginary line drawn through points on the earth's surface where the magnetic deviation is equal.

JOULE.—A unit of energy or work. A joule of energy is liberated by one ampere flowing for one second through a resistance of one ohm.

KILO.—A prefix meaning 1,000.

LAG.—The amount one wave is behind another in time; expressed in electrical degrees.

LAMINATED CORE.—A core built up from thin sheets of metal and used in transformers and relays.

LEAD.—The opposite of LAG. Also, a wire or connection.

ELECTRICAL TERMS AND FORMULAS

LINE OF FORCE.—A line in an electric or magnetic field that shows the direction of the force.

LOAD.—The power that is being delivered by any power producing device. The equipment that uses the power from the power producing device.

MAGNETIC AMPLIFIER.—A saturable reactor type device that is used in a circuit to amplify or control.

MAGNETIC CIRCUIT.—The complete path of magnetic lines of force.

MAGNETIC FIELD.—The space in which a magnetic force exists.

MAGNETIC FLUX.—The total number of lines of force issuing from a pole of a magnet.

MAGNETIZE.—To convert a material into a magnet by causing the molecules to rearrange.

MAGNETO.—A generator which produces alternating current and has a permanent magnet as its field.

MEGGER.—A test instrument used to measure insulation resistance and other high resistances. It is a portable hand operated d-c generator used as an ohmmeter.

MEGOHM.—A million ohms.

MICRO.—A prefix meaning one-millionth.

MILLI.—A prefix meaning one-thousandth.

MILLIAMMETER.—An ammeter that measures current in thousandths of an ampere.

MOTOR-GENERATOR.—A motor and a generator with a common shaft used to convert line voltages to other voltages or frequencies.

MUTUAL INDUCTANCE.—A circuit property existing when the relative position of two inductors causes the magnetic lines of force from one to link with the turns of the other.

NEGATIVE CHARGE.—The electrical charge carried by a body which has an excess of electrons.

NEUTRON.—A particle having the weight of a proton but carrying no electric charge. It is located in the nucleus of an atom.

NUCLEUS.—The central part of an atom that is mainly comprised of protons and neutrons. It is the part of the atom that has the most mass.

NULL.—Zero.

OHM.—The unit of electrical resistance.

OHMMETER.—An instrument for directly measuring resistance in ohms.

OVERLOAD.—A load greater than the rated load of an electrical device.

PERMALLOY.—An alloy of nickel and iron having an abnormally high magnetic permeability.

PERMEABILITY.—A measure of the ease with which magnetic lines of force can flow through a material as compared to air.

PHASE DIFFERENCE.—The time in electrical degrees by which one wave leads or lags another.

POLARITY.—The character of having magnetic poles, or electric charges.

POLE.—The section of a magnet where the flux lines are concentrated; also where they enter and leave the magnet. An electrode of a battery.

POLYPHASE.—A circuit that utilizes more than one phase of alternating current.

POSITIVE CHARGE.—The electrical charge carried by a body which has become deficient in electrons.

POTENTIAL.—The amount of charge held by a body as compared to another point or body. Usually measured in volts.

POTENTIOMETER.—A variable voltage divider; a resistor which has a variable contact arm so that any portion of the potential applied between its ends may be selected.

POWER.—The rate of doing work or the rate of expending energy. The unit of electrical power is the watt.

POWER FACTOR.—The ratio of the actual power of an alternating or pulsating current, as measured by a wattmeter, to the apparent power, as indicated by ammeter and voltmeter readings. The power factor of an inductor, capacitor, or insulator is an expression of their losses.

PRIME MOVER.—The source of mechanical power used to drive the rotor of a generator.

PROTON.—A positively charged particle in the nucleus of an atom.

RATIO.—The value obtained by dividing one number by another, indicating their relative proportions.

REACTANCE.—The opposition offered to the flow of an alternating current by the inductance, capacitance, or both, in any circuit.

RECTIFIERS.—Devices used to change alternating current to unidirectional current. These may be vacuum tubes, semiconductors such as germanium and silicon, and dry-disk rectifiers such as selenium and copper-oxide.

RELAY.—An electromechanical switching device that can be used as a remote control.

RELUCTANCE.—A measure of the opposition that a material offers to magnetic lines of force.

RESISTANCE.—The opposition to the flow of current caused by the nature and physical dimensions of a conductor.

RESISTOR.—A circuit element whose chief characteristic is resistance; used to oppose the flow of current.

ELECTRICAL TERMS AND FORMULAS

RETENTIVITY.—The measure of the ability of a material to hold its magnetism.

RHEOSTAT.—A variable resistor.

SATURABLE REACTOR.—A control device that uses a small d-c current to control a large a-c current by controlling core flux density.

SATURATION.—The condition existing in any circuit when an increase in the driving signal produces no further change in the resultant effect.

SELF-INDUCTION.—The process by which a circuit induces an e.m.f. into itself by its own magnetic field.

SERIES-WOUND.—A motor or generator in which the armature is wired in series with the field winding.

SERVO.—A device used to convert a small movement into one of greater movement or force.

SERVOMECHANISM.—A closed-loop system that produces a force to position an object in accordance with the information that originates at the input.

SOLENOID.—An electromagnetic coil that contains a movable plunger.

SPACE CHARGE.—The cloud of electrons existing in the space between the cathode and plate in a vacuum tube, formed by the electrons emitted from the cathode in excess of those immediately attracted to the plate.

SPECIFIC GRAVITY—The ratio between the density of a substance and that of pure water, at a given temperature.

SYNCHROSCOPE—An instrument used to indicate a difference in frequency between two a-c sources.

SYNCHRO SYSTEM.—An electrical system that gives remote indications or control by means of self-synchronizing motors.

TACHOMETER.—An instrument for indicating revolutions per minute.

TERTIARY WINDING.—A third winding on a transformer or magnetic amplifier that is used as a second control winding.

THERMISTOR.—A resistor that is used to compensate for temperature variations in a circuit.

THERMOCOUPLE.—A junction of two dissimilar metals that produces a voltage when heated.

TORQUE.—The turning effort or twist which a shaft sustains when transmitting power.

TRANSFORMER.—A device composed of two or more coils, linked by magnetic lines of force, used to transfer energy from one circuit to another.

TRANSMISSION LINES.—Any conductor or system of conductors used to carry electrical energy from its source to a load.

VARS.—Abbreviation for volt-ampere, reactive.

VECTOR.—A line used to represent both direction and magnitude.

VOLT.—The unit of electrical potential.

VOLTMETER.—An instrument designed to measure a difference in electrical potential, in volts.

WATT.—The unit of electrical power.

WATTMETER.—An instrument for measuring electrical power in watts.

Formulas

Ohm's Law for d-c Circuits

$$I = \frac{E}{R} = \frac{P}{E} = \sqrt{\frac{P}{R}}$$

$$R = \frac{E}{I} = \frac{P}{I^2} = \frac{E^2}{P}$$

$$E = IR = \frac{P}{I} = \sqrt{PR}$$

$$P = EI = \frac{E^2}{R} = I^2R$$

Resistors in Series

$$R_T = R_1 + R_2 \ldots$$

Resistors in Parallel

Two resistors

$$R_T = \frac{R_1 R_2}{R_1 + R_2}$$

More than two

$$\frac{1}{R_T} = \frac{1}{R_1} + \frac{1}{R_2} + \frac{1}{R_3}$$

ELECTRICAL TERMS AND FORMULAS

R-L Circuit Time Constant equals

$$\frac{L \text{ (in henrys)}}{R \text{ (in ohms)}} = t \text{ (in seconds), or}$$

$$\frac{L \text{ (in microhenrys)}}{R \text{ (in ohms)}} = t \text{ (in microseconds)}$$

R-C Circuit Time Constant equals
R (ohms) X C (farads) = t (seconds)
R (megohms) x C (microfarads) = t (seconds)
R (ohms) x C (microfarads) = t (microseconds)
R (megohms) x C (micromicrofrads = t (microseconds)

Comparison of Units in Electric and Magnetic Circuits.

	Electric circuit	Magnetic circuit
Force	Volt, E or e.m.f.	Gilberts, F, or m.m.f.
Flow	Ampere, I	Flux, Φ, in maxwells
Opposition	Ohms, R	Reluctance, R
Law	Ohm's law, $I = \frac{E}{R}$	Rowland's law $\Phi = \frac{F}{R}$
Intensity of force	Volts per cm. of length	$H = \frac{1.257 IN}{L}$, gilberts per centimeter of length
Density	Current density— for example, amperes per cm^2.	Flux density—for example, lines per cm^2., or gausses

Capacitors in Series
Two capacitors

$$C_T = \frac{C_1 C_2}{C_1 + C_2}$$

More than two

$$\frac{1}{C_T} = \frac{1}{C_1} + \frac{1}{C_2} + \frac{1}{C_3}...$$

Capacitors in Parallel

$$C_T = C_1 + C_2 ...$$

Capacitive Reactance

$$X_c = \frac{1}{2\pi f C}$$

Impedance in an R-C Circuit (Series)

$$Z = \sqrt{R^2 + X_c^2}$$

Inductors in Series

$$L_T = L_1 + L_2 ... \text{ (No coupling between coils)}$$

Inductors in Parallel
Two inductors

$$L_T = \frac{L_1 L_2}{L_1 + L_2} \text{ (No coupling between coils)}$$

More than two

$$\frac{1}{L_T} = \frac{1}{L_1} + \frac{1}{L_2} + \frac{1}{L_3} ... \text{ (No coupling between coils)}$$

Inductive Reactance

$$X_L = 2\pi f L$$

Q of a Coil

$$Q = \frac{X_L}{R}$$

Impedance of an R-L Circuit (series)

$$Z = \sqrt{R^2 + X_L^2}$$

Impedance with R, C, and L in Series

$$Z = \sqrt{R^2 + (X_L - X_C)^2}$$

Parallel Circuit Impedance

$$Z = \frac{Z_1 Z_2}{Z_1 + Z_2}$$

Sine-Wave Voltage Relationships
Average value

$$E_{ave} = \frac{2}{\pi} \times E_{max} = 0.637 E_{max}$$

ELECTRICAL TERMS AND FORMULAS

Effective or r.m.s. value

$$E_{eff} = \frac{E_{max}}{\sqrt{2}} = \frac{E_{max}}{1.414} = 0.707 E_{max} = 1.11 E_{ave}$$

Maximum value

$$E_{max} = \sqrt{2} E_{eff} = 1.414 E_{eff} = 1.57 E_{ave}$$

Voltage in an a-c circuit

$$E = IZ = \frac{P}{I \times P.F.}$$

Current in an a-c circuit

$$I = \frac{E}{Z} = \frac{P}{E \times P.F.}$$

Power in A-C Circuit
  Apparent power = EI
  True power

$$P = EI \cos \theta = EI \times P.F.$$

Power factor

$$P.F. = \frac{P}{EI} = \cos \theta$$

$$\cos \theta = \frac{\text{true power}}{\text{apparent power}}$$

Transformers
  Voltage relationship

$$\frac{E}{E} = \frac{N}{N} \text{ or } E = E \times \frac{N}{N}$$

  Current relationship

$$\frac{I_p}{I_s} = \frac{N_s}{N_p}$$

Induced voltage

$$E_{eff} = 4.44 \, BAfN \times 10^{-8}$$

Turns ratio equals

$$\frac{N_p}{N_s} = \sqrt{\frac{Z_p}{Z_s}}$$

Secondary current

$$I_s = I_p \frac{N_p}{N_s}$$

Secondary voltage

$$E_s = E_p \frac{N_s}{N_p}$$

Three Phase Voltage and Current Relationships
With wye connected windings

$$E_{line} = 1.732 E_{coil} = \sqrt{3} E_{coil}$$

$$I_{line} = I_{coil}$$

With delta connected windings

$$E_{line} = E_{coil}$$

$$I_{line} = 1.732 I_{coil}$$

With wye or delta connected winding

$$P_{coil} = E_{coil} I_{coil}$$

$$P_t = 3 P_{coil}$$

$$P_t = 1.732 E_{line} I_{line}$$

(To convert to true power multiply by $\cos \theta$)

Synchronous Speed of Motor

$$r.p.m. = \frac{120 \times \text{frequency}}{\text{number of poles}}$$

GREEK ALPHABET

Name	Capital	Lower Case	Designates
Alpha	A	α	Angles.
Beta	B	β	Angles, flux density.
Gamma	Γ	γ	Conductivity.
Delta	Δ	δ	Variation of a quantity, increment.
Epsilon	E	ε	Base of natural logarithms (2.71828).
Zeta	Z	ζ	Impedance, coefficients, coordinates.
Eta	H	η	Hysteresis coefficient, efficiency, magnetizing force.
Theta	Θ	θ	Phase angle.
Iota	I	ι	
Kappa	K	κ	Dielectric constant, coupling coefficient, susceptibility.
Lambda	Λ	λ	Wavelength.
Mu	M	μ	Permeability, micro, amplification factor.
Nu	N	ν	Reluctivity.
Xi	Ξ	ξ	
Omicron	O	ο	
Pi	Π	π	3.1416
Rho	P	ρ	Resistivity.
Sigma	Σ	σ	
Tau	T	τ	Time constant, time-phase displacement.
Upsilon	Υ	υ	
Phi	Φ	φ	Angles, magnetic flux.
Chi	X	χ	
Psi	Ψ	ψ	Dielectric flux, phase difference.
Omega	Ω	ω	Ohms (capital), angular velocity ($2\pi f$).

COMMON ABBREVIATIONS AND LETTER SYMBOLS

Term	Abbreviation or Symbol
alternating current (noun)	a.c.
alternating-current (adj.)	a-c
ampere	a.
area	A
audiofrequency (noun)	AF
audiofrequency (adj.)	A-F
capacitance	C
capacitive reactance	X_C
centimeter	cm.
conductance	G
coulomb	Q
counterelectromotive force	c.e.m.f.
current (d-c or r.m.s. value)	I
current (instantaneous value)	i
cycles per second	c.p.s.
dielectric constant	K,k
difference in potential (d-c or r.m.s. value)	E
difference in potential (instantaneous value)	e
direct current (noun)	d.c.
direct-current (adj.)	d-c
electromotive force	e.m.f.
frequency	f
henry	h.
horsepower	hp.
impedance	Z
inductance	L
inductive reactance	X_L
kilovolt	kv.
kilovolt-ampere	kv.-a.
kilowatt	kw.
kilowatt-hour	kw.-hr.
magnetic field intensity	H
magnetomotive force	m.m.f.
megohm	M
microampere	μ a.
microfarad	μ f.
microhenry	μ h.
micromicrofarad	$\mu\mu$ f.
microvolt	μ v.
milliampere	ma.
millihenry	mh.
milliwatt	mw.
mutual inductance	M
power	P
resistance	R
revolutions per minute	r.p.m.
root mean square	r.m.s.
time	t
torque	T
volt	v.
watt	w.

www.ingramcontent.com/pod-product-compliance
Lightning Source LLC
Chambersburg PA
CBHW081819300426
44116CB00014B/2416